COMBATING HUMAN TRAFFICKING IN CHINA: DOMESTIC AND INTERNATIONAL EFFORTS

United States Congress Senate

The BiblioGov Project is an effort to expand awareness of the public documents and records of the U.S. Government via print publications. In broadening the public understanding of government and its work, an enlightened democracy can grow and prosper. Ranging from historic Congressional Bills to the most recent Budget of the United States Government, the BiblioGov Project spans a wealth of government information. These works are now made available through an environmentally friendly, print-on-demand basis, using only what is necessary to meet the required demands of an interested public. We invite you to learn of the records of the U.S. Government, heightening the knowledge and debate that can lead from such publications.

Included are the following Collections:

Budget of The United States Government
Presidential Documents
United States Code
Education Reports from ERIC
GAO Reports
History of Bills
House Rules and Manual
Public and Private Laws

Code of Federal Regulations
Congressional Documents
Economic Indicators
Federal Register
Government Manuals
House Journal
Privacy act Issuances
Statutes at Large

COMBATING HUMAN TRAFFICKING IN CHINA: DOMESTIC AND INTERNATIONAL EFFORTS

HEARING

BEFORE THE

CONGRESSIONAL-EXECUTIVE COMMISSION ON CHINA

ONE HUNDRED NINTH CONGRESS

SECOND SESSION

MARCH 6, 2006

Printed for the use of the Congressional-Executive Commission on China

Available via the World Wide Web: http://www.cecc.gov

U.S. GOVERNMENT PRINTING OFFICE

26–671 PDF   WASHINGTON : 2006

For sale by the Superintendent of Documents, U.S. Government Printing Office
Internet: bookstore.gpo.gov   Phone: toll free (866) 512–1800; DC area (202) 512–1800
Fax: (202) 512–2250   Mail: Stop SSOP, Washington, DC 20402–0001

CONGRESSIONAL-EXECUTIVE COMMISSION ON CHINA

LEGISLATIVE BRANCH COMMISSIONERS

Senate

CHUCK HAGEL, Nebraska, *Chairman*
SAM BROWNBACK, Kansas
GORDON SMITH, Oregon
JIM DeMINT, South Carolina
MEL MARTINEZ, Florida
MAX BAUCUS, Montana
CARL LEVIN, Michigan
DIANNE FEINSTEIN, California
BYRON DORGAN, North Dakota

House

JAMES A. LEACH, Iowa, *Co-Chairman*
DAVID DREIER, California
FRANK R. WOLF, Virginia
JOSEPH R. PITTS, Pennsylvania
ROBERT B. ADERHOLT, Alabama
SANDER LEVIN, Michigan
MARCY KAPTUR, Ohio
SHERROD BROWN, Ohio
MICHAEL M. HONDA, California

EXECUTIVE BRANCH COMMISSIONERS

STEVEN J. LAW, Department of Labor
PAULA DOBRIANSKY, Department of State

DAVID DORMAN, *Staff Director (Chairman)*
JOHN FOARDE, *Staff Director (Co-Chairman)*

CONTENTS

Page

STATEMENTS

Opening statement of Hon. Chuck Hagel, a U.S. Senator from Nebraska, Chairman, Congressional-Executive Commission on China 1
Leach, Hon. James A., a U.S. Representative from Iowa, Co-chairman, Congressional-Executive Commission on China 3
Law, Steven J., Deputy Secretary, U.S. Department of Labor, Member, Congressional-Executive Commission on China 4
Smith, Hon. Christopher H., a U.S. Representative from New Jersey 5
Miller, Hon. John R., Ambassador-at-Large and Director, Office to Monitor and Combat Trafficking in Persons, U.S. Department of State; accompanied by Mark B. Taylor, Senior Coordinator, Reports Office to Monitor and Combat Trafficking in Persons, Washington, DC 8
Plant, Roger, Head, Special Action Program to Combat Forced Labor, International Labor Organization, Geneva, Switzerland 17
Perkins, Wenchi Yu, Director, Anti-Trafficking and Human Rights Program, Vital Voices, Washington, DC 22
Lee, Abraham, Director of Public Relations, Crossing Borders, College Park, MD 25

APPENDIX

Prepared Statements

Smith, Hon. Christopher H 36
Miller, Hon. John R 38
Plant, Roger 40
Perkins, Wenchi Yu 44
Lee, Abraham 49
Hagel, Hon. Chuck 52
Leach, Hon. James A 54
Brownback, Hon. Sam, a U.S. Senator from Kansas, Member, Congressional-Executive Commission on China 54
Law, Hon. Steven J 56

COMBATING HUMAN TRAFFICKING IN CHINA: DOMESTIC AND INTERNATIONAL EFFORTS

MONDAY, MARCH 6, 2006

CONGRESSIONAL-EXECUTIVE
COMMISSION ON CHINA,
Washington, DC.

The hearing was convened, pursuant to notice, at 2:05 p.m., in room 419, Dirksen Senate Office Building, Senator Chuck Hagel (Chairman of the Commission) presiding.

Also present: Representative Jim Leach, Co-Chairman; Representative Sander M. Levin; and Steven J. Law, Deputy Secretary, U.S. Department of Labor.

OPENING STATEMENT OF HON. CHUCK HAGEL, A U.S. SENATOR FROM NEBRASKA, CHAIRMAN, CONGRESSIONAL-EXECUTIVE COMMISSION ON CHINA

Chairman HAGEL. Good afternoon. Welcome.

The Congressional-Executive Commission on China meets today to examine human trafficking in China. The Commission will also consider domestic and international efforts to help stop human trafficking in and through China, and to help rehabilitate victims of trafficking.

Human trafficking in China is a serious problem. According to a 2002 UNICEF estimate, there are approximately 250,000 victims of trafficking in China. Traffickers are increasingly linked to organized crime, and specialize in abducting girls and women, both for the bridal market in China's poorest areas, and for sale as prostitutes in urban areas. North Korean refugees are an especially vulnerable group.

Today's Administration witness, Ambassador John Miller, has estimated that 80 to 90 percent of the refugees from North Korea, particularly women and children, end up as trafficking victims.

The Chinese Government has publicly acknowledged the seriousness of the problem and taken steps to stop trafficking and aid victims. Chinese experts and officials have cooperated with international agencies, including the ILO and UNICEF, to combat trafficking.

China's law on the protection of rights and interests of women outlaws trafficking, as does Article 240 of the Criminal Law, and outlines harsh penalties for those convicted of human trafficking-related crimes.

These steps reflect a serious effort, but the Chinese Government needs to do far more. The Commission is concerned that China fell from Tier 2 to Tier 2 Watch Status in the State Department's

"Trafficking in Persons Report" in 2005 because of inadequate protection of trafficking victims.

The Chinese Government must uphold international agreements and grant the U.N. High Commissioner for Refugees unimpeded access to screen the refugee petitions of North Koreans in China.

The Chinese Government has not signed the U.N. Protocol to Prevent, Suppress, and Punish Trafficking in Persons, Especially Women and Children.

The United States can also do more. In its 2005 Annual Report, the Commission recommended that the President and Congress continue to support international programs to build law enforcement capacity to prevent trafficking in and through China, and additionally should develop and fund programs led by U.S.-based NGOs that focus on the protection and rehabilitation of victims, especially legal and educational assistance programs. But the Chinese Government must become more open to cooperation with foreign NGO groups. To help us better understand the human trafficking problem in China, and international and domestic efforts to fight trafficking and assist victims, we turn to our witnesses today.

Representative Chris Smith has been a leader in Congressional efforts to combat trafficking worldwide and to assist victims of trafficking. Earlier this year, President Bush signed into law Representative Smith's third anti-trafficking bill, the Trafficking Victims Protection Reauthorization Act of 2005. This new law provides significant additional anti-trafficking and protection measures for victims and potential victims of trafficking. Representative Smith is Vice Chairman of the House International Relations Committee and Chairman of the International Relations Subcommittee on Africa, Global Human Rights, and International Operations. The Commission is very pleased that Mr. Smith will be making a statement at today's hearing.

Speaking on behalf of the Administration will be Ambassador John Miller, who is Director of the State Department's Office to Monitor and Combat Trafficking in Persons, and Senior Advisor to Secretary of State Condoleeza Rice on Human Trafficking. From 1985 to 1993, Mr. Miller served in the U.S. House of Representatives from the State of Washington. While in Congress, Mr. Miller held a seat on the Committee on International Relations, and was a member of the Congressional Human Rights Caucus.

After Ambassador Miller, we will hear from a distinguished panel of experts who will share their knowledge and expertise. Mr. Roger Plant will lead panel three. Mr. Plant is the head of the ILO's Special Action Program to Combat Forced Labor. Mr. Plant has been a leading investigator and activist on forced labor and modern slavery for more than 30 years. Prior to joining the ILO, Mr. Plant worked with the Asian Development Bank, United Kingdom Department for International Development, Inter-American Development Bank, the United Nations Office of the High Commissioner for Human Rights, Shell International, Danish International Development Agency, and several international human rights NGOs.

Ms. Wenchi Yu Perkins will provide perspectives on the problem of human trafficking to and from China. Ms. Perkins is the Director of Anti-Trafficking and Human Rights Programs at Vital

Voices. Prior to joining Vital Voices, Ms. Perkins worked with victims of trafficking and conducted training for law enforcement and NGOs in the Midwest. She was also a foreign policy assistant in Taiwan's legislature, and worked in the Taiwan Economic and Cultural Representative's office in Chicago. She has an M.A. in International Relations from the University of Chicago, and a B.A. in Political Science from National Taiwan University.

Finally, Mr. Abraham Lee will testify to the Commission on the problems faced by North Korean refugees in China. Mr. Lee is Director of Public Affairs for Crossing Borders, a non-governmental organization devoted to assisting North Korean refugees in northeast China. Mr. Lee has been in China for the past three years, working with North Korean refugees and teaching college English. He received his B.A. in Economics from the University of Maryland in 1999, and his J.D. from the Maryland School of Law in 2002.

We welcome all of our witnesses today and appreciate their time and presentations.

Before we begin with Congressman Smith, I would ask the Co-Chairman of the Commission, Mr. Leach, a senior member of the House International Relations Committee from the State of Iowa, if he would like to make a presentation. Then after Congressman Leach, I would ask the Deputy Secretary of Labor, Mr. Law, if he would care to make a statement. Congressman Leach.

STATEMENT OF HON. JAMES A. LEACH, A U.S. REPRESENTATIVE FROM IOWA, CO-CHAIRMAN, CONGRESSIONAL-EXECUTIVE COMMISSION ON CHINA

Representative LEACH. Mr. Chairman, I would just ask unanimous consent to put my statement in the record.

Chairman HAGEL. Without objection, it will be placed in the record.

Representative LEACH. I am, and I am sure I speak for all of us, deeply honored that Chris Smith has joined us today. Chris is really an acknowledged expert on this subject, and our House's strongest moral voice on issues of this nature. We appreciate your coming, Chris.

John Miller, our colleague, has longstanding expertise on these issues as well, and has served with great distinction at the State Department. We appreciate you are with us now as an ambassador, John.

With regard to the issue, I think it is important to note that the problems are truly profound, but China has taken some modest steps. Some 25,000 people have been arrested over a three-year period, from 2002 to 2004, and laws have been improved. On the other hand, it is not clear that the Chinese Government has paid as great attention to enforcement as should be the case. In fact, that would be an understatement. When you have a quarter of a million women that seem to be in jeopardy in human trafficking in a given country, that is an extraordinary thing that the world community cannot ignore.

We as a Congress are particularly sensitive to the North Korean refugee issue, which is one of the great dilemmas of modern times. The notion that a people would vote with their feet to become trafficked really underscores the dilemma of North Korea itself, so we have to really be attentive to that.

Thank you, Mr. Chairman.

[The prepared statement of Representative Leach appears in the appendix.]

Chairman HAGEL. Congressman Leach, thank you.

Deputy Secretary of Labor, Mr. Law.

STATEMENT OF STEVEN J. LAW, DEPUTY SECRETARY, U.S. DEPARTMENT OF LABOR, MEMBER, CONGRESSIONAL-EXECUTIVE COMMISSION ON CHINA

Mr. LAW. Thank you. I also have a written statement for the record that I ask unanimous consent to have placed in that record.

Chairman HAGEL. Without objection, it will be placed in the record.

Mr. LAW. I will just abbreviate those comments.

First, I want to commend the Chairman and the staff of the Commission for organizing this important hearing today on the timely subject of human trafficking in China.

This Commission has an important mandate to not only study and report on human rights issues in China, but also to visibly highlight those issues and offer constructive policy responses for the benefit of the Executive Branch and the Legislative Branch.

As we all know, there is tremendous ferment in the People's Republic of China, and most of the developments that we see have to do with economic growth and change. But China's rapid economic growth also raises a broad array of other pressing issues—many internal and many with global implications.

Increasingly, we see issues such as human rights, worker protections, open access to the Internet, and intellectual property rights all moving to the front burner in China, and even converging at various points.

One of the most consequential facts of life in this rapidly developing nation is the mass migration of its people to urban and industrialized areas in search of economic opportunity. That is not necessarily a bad change.

But when there is such rapid movement of people, especially people who are economically and socially vulnerable, people who are moving from safe, familiar communities to anonymous, unfamiliar destinations, that is where the potential for exploitation arises. And, of course, there is no more heinous form of exploitation than human trafficking.

President George W. Bush has called human trafficking a "modern form of slavery" and has committed his Administration to the fight against this global scandal. Just over a month ago, in part because of the tremendous work of our first witness, Congressman Smith, the President signed into law the Trafficking Victims Protection Reauthorization Act, strengthening U.S. Government efforts to combat human trafficking, both here and abroad.

Over the last 10 years, the Department of Labor has invested over $164 million in projects worldwide that are designed to stop human trafficking for the purposes of forced labor and commercial sexual exploitation.

Today, we will be focusing on a critical question: just how pervasive is the problem of human trafficking today in China? At the same time, regardless of whether the problem is as widespread in China today as it is in some other countries, we need to note the confluence of conditions that make China especially vulnerable to the growth of human trafficking in its future: its enormous population, the mass migration of people within its borders and across its borders, pockets of dire economic need in some parts of the country, and its proximity to other nations where human trafficking is pervasive.

There are significant cultural factors as well that contribute to human trafficking pressures. For example, there are continuing reports of forced marriage and the unique pressures created by the Chinese Government's one child policy all increase the likelihood that China may develop a serious human trafficking problem—if proactive steps are not taken now to prevent that from happening.

In the last few years, the Chinese Government has stepped forward to address a range of human rights and worker rights issues, and the U.S. Department of Labor has provided technical support and other assistance for these welcome efforts.

We at the Department of Labor look forward to working with China and the non-governmental organization community to help shape effective national policies, gather reliable data, and pursue aggressive law enforcement strategies to overcome this problem in China.

Thank you, Mr. Chairman.

[The prepared statement of Mr. Law appears in the appendix.]

Chairman HAGEL. Secretary Law, thank you.

Congressman Smith, welcome. We are glad you are here.

STATEMENT OF HON. CHRISTOPHER H. SMITH, A U.S. REPRESENTATIVE FROM NEW JERSEY

Representative SMITH. Mr. Chairman, thank you so much for the very kind introduction, and to all three of you for the extraordinary work you are doing on behalf of the people of China, especially its victims. You stand with the oppressed and not the oppressor, and I think you are to be greatly congratulated for that.

To Congressman Leach, with whom we have had a number of hearings together, joint hearings on issues relevant to China, to North Korea—we had two last year—thank you for your kind words. I feel very much indebted to your fine work on behalf of human rights around the globe, but especially in China.

This hearing is particularly timely. I would ask unanimous consent that my full statement be made part of the record.

Chairman HAGEL. Without objection, it will be included in the record.

Representative SMITH. I thank you, Mr. Chairman.

This hearing is particularly timely. A BBC report in January 2006 indicates that China may replace Thailand in the next few years as the region's trafficking hub, all at a time when the age of victims being trafficked is falling. With too much frequency, we now read news accounts, as well as NGO reporting, of women and girls being abducted in places like Burma, North Korea, and Vietnam, who are then trafficked and sold into slavery into the People's Republic of China.

We all know that China has a myriad of human rights abuses, in addition to repression of religious freedom and political freedom. Mr. Leach and I just co-chaired a hearing that went for about seven hours just a couple of weeks ago on the new crackdown on the Internet and the use of the Internet, especially by the public security police, to find, apprehend, incarcerate, and then eventually torture in the laogai system those who believe in human rights and freedom, and those who are promoting religious freedom as well. So there is this all-encompassing repression which we see in China, notwithstanding the strides that have been made in the area of economic freedom.

I would like to offer, in addition to what I think many of our witnesses will offer, some of the reasons for this growth of trafficking in China.

In addition to the proliferation of gangs, the huge amounts of money that are to be made by trafficking women, by turning women into commodities, is not unlike drug trafficking, which continues to be the biggest moneymaker. We now know that human trafficking is probably number two in terms of moneymakers for international organized crime. Regrettably, this exploitation of women is done over and over again, as the victim is exploited and raped, and the money that is made or gleaned from it puts more money into the traffickers' pockets.

But I would like to offer an additional couple of reasons—at least one, maybe two—as to why this issue in China is unique. I would offer to my friends and colleagues that if we ask why so many women now are being trafficked into China, since 1979, I think, as members know, the People's Republic of China has imposed and implemented a cruel policy that has systematically rendered children illegal and "dead" unless authorized by what they call a birth allowance certificate. The "one child per couple" policy imposes ruinous fines, up to 10 times both the husband and wife's salary, for a child who is conceived outside of a government plan. As a direct result of these ongoing crimes against humanity, China today is missing girls, girls who are murdered simply because they are girls—gendercide.

A couple of years ago, the State Department suggested that as many 100 million girls of all ages are missing. That is to say, they should be alive and well somewhere in China, but are not, a direct consequence of the one child policy.

China is the only country in the world whose systematic human rights abuses touch virtually every chapter without exception. It results in the mass killing of people based exclusively on their gender. Gendercide, in fact, constitutes one of humanity's worst blights.

Let me just point out to my colleagues, and I have given you a copy of just one report that was from about a year ago, March 9, 2004, that was in The Guardian newspaper. It points out that there may be as many as 40 million single men by the year 2020 who are looking for wives and cannot find them because of the one child policy, creating a shortage of female babies. It points out what Li Weixiang, who advises the Chinese People's Political Consultative Conference on population issues, said at a conference: "This is by no means a sensational prediction, and that it will lead to a dramatic rise in prostitution and in the trafficking of women."

Let me just hope that my colleagues, especially on this Commission, will begin to look at the nexus between the "one child per couple policy" and this gendercide and the issue of trafficking.

When there is such a dearth of women, of girls who are of marriageable age, the men will begin looking somewhere else. We now hear increasing stories of slave wives, where there will be one wife for several men. The pressure will only increase as this lack of girls or women goes through the demographic system in China. You will see increasing pressure, if you will, for trafficked girls from all over the world, especially from neighboring countries.

Let me also point out that there is a very serious impact to women themselves that also creates pressure for trafficking. That is, as a direct result of the one child policy, it is estimated that female suicides are increasing, five times the average of any other country in the world. About 500 women commit suicide in China each and every day. Not per week, not per month, but per day. That is a very frightening statistic, but it also creates a demand for more trafficked women.

Another important issue that I would like to spend just a moment on is the issue of China's contravention of the Refugee Convention as it relates to North Korean refugees, who make it across the border line only to be trafficked. Last October, I chaired a hearing on the horrific problem, along with my friend and colleague Mr. Leach, of North Koreans who are trafficked in China. Mrs. Cha Syeong Sook told us how the food distribution center in P'yongyang stopped distributing food at the end of June 1995.

In October 1997, she jumped into the Tumen River to find her daughter, who had gone to China looking for food. Much later, she found out, all Chinese living close to the border were involved in human trafficking. They bought and sold North Korean girls, with the help of North Koreans. Mrs. Cha was hired by a man in Hwa Ryong city, along with several other North Korean women who were regularly raped. Another man bought her daughter for about $400, and they worked for him as servants in his home. They escaped again, but were eventually kidnapped by human traffickers two months later.

Eventually, Mrs. Cha and her daughter were sent by the Chinese police to the North Korean detention center, where she found out that her second daughter had been trafficked. Mrs. Cha and her three children finally found their way to South Korea in a long, arduous journey. But they are just the tip of the iceberg of those who escape the perils of North Korea, only to find themselves victims of trafficking once they make it inside the borders of the People's Republic of China.

Mr. Chairman, again, I ask that my full statement be made a part of the record. But I really hope we begin to focus renewed attention on China as it relates to trafficking. They are now, as you pointed out correctly, a Tier 2 Watch List country. I happen to believe, based on the overwhelming amount of evidence, just as they are considered countries of particular concern because of their ongoing and egregious human rights abuses vis-a-vis religious freedom, when it comes to trafficking they have done far too little to effectuate the release, the protection, and the prosecution of those who traffic.

The number of traffic cases where prosecution has been forthcoming, and as the Ambassador I think will point out, we do not know how many are actually convicted. We get arrest numbers. We get the number of people who are apprehended, we do not get the number of people who go to jail for trafficking individuals. So, that is another, I think, very notable missing element in their reporting and their providing us data on what they are doing to combat this terrible crime.

So, Mr. Chairman, I think this hearing is very timely. But I urge you, I urge this Commission, to look at the nexus again between the one child policy, the dearth of girls, girl babies, girl children, and this ballooning problem of human trafficking in the PRC.

I thank you.

[The prepared statement of Representative Smith appears in the appendix.]

Chairman HAGEL. Congressman Smith, thank you very, very much.

We have been joined by another of your colleagues, Congressman Levin. Before you leave, Congressman Smith, let me ask any of the Members of the Commission if they would wish to address any point you have made.

Congressman Leach?

Representative LEACH. I just would like to observe that Mr. Smith has gone to Washington, stayed, and done a remarkable job.

Representative SMITH. Thanks, Jim.

Chairman HAGEL. Mr. Smith, thank you very much.

Representative SMITH. Thank you very much, Mr. Chairman.

Chairman HAGEL. Ambassador Miller, thank you. Ambassador Miller, welcome. We are very pleased you are here and look forward to your testimony.

STATEMENT OF HON. JOHN R. MILLER, AMBASSADOR-AT-LARGE AND DIRECTOR, OFFICE TO MONITOR AND COMBAT TRAFFICKING IN PERSONS, U.S. DEPARTMENT OF STATE; ACCOMPANIED BY MARK B. TAYLOR, SENIOR COORDINATOR, REPORTS, OFFICE TO MONITOR AND COMBAT TRAFFICKING IN PERSONS, U.S. DEPARTMENT OF STATE, WASHINGTON, DC

Mr. MILLER. Well, Chairman Hagel, Deputy Secretary Law, my former colleagues, Congressmen Leach and Levin, it is good to be here with you today. I appreciate your addressing the subject of what we euphemistically call trafficking in persons in China. I say "euphemistically," because we use that phrase all over the world, but of course, we are talking about the slave trade.

If you have no objections, I have a formal statement that I would like entered in the record.

Chairman HAGEL. It will be included in the record.

Thank you.

Mr. MILLER. You have many distinguished witnesses today. Congressman Smith, a leader on this issue, has already testified. You are going to hear from Roger Plant of the ILO, with whom we have worked in China, and Wenchi Yu Perkins of Vital Voices. We have also worked with Abraham Lee, who has been on the ground in China and South Korea, and can bring some first-hand observations. So, I will not take long.

I have traveled all over the world on this issue. I have been to China. My colleague here, Mark Taylor, head of our Reports section, was in China for several days just a month ago.

Of course, we are talking about a worldwide challenge. Slavery affects every country in the world, as far as I am concerned, including the United States of America. In the world context, we are looking at, our government estimates, up to 800,000 men, women and children trafficked across international borders every year. That is just across international borders. That is not counting internal trafficking.

There are many categories of trafficking around the world. The largest category probably is sex slavery. The second-largest category is probably domestic servitude slavery. Then you have factory slavery, which Deputy Secretary Law is familiar with, farm slavery, and child soldier slavery, even child camel jockey slavery in parts of the Middle East.

You have here a worldwide challenge that affects not only human rights and the dignity of individuals, but it is a public health challenge, and a national security challenge because of the link to organized crime.

Now, turning to China, I think before even getting into the limited information we have on China, one has to start out with a qualification. Because of the lack of openness in China, we do not have as much information. We have not talked with the victims who we are able to talk with in many other countries. Generally, when I visit a country I always talk with victims. In China, I was there for a couple of days. I did not talk with victims. My colleague, Mr. Taylor, made an effort in one part of China to talk with victims, but it is not easy to do. China does not have a lot of NGOs working on this issue. There is an All China Women's Federation, a government NGO, but it is difficult for NGOs that are independent or from abroad to work on this issue. You have discussed the Internet, I believe, Congressman Leach, at a recent hearing. Our State Department Web site, I am told by our Embassy, that has a trafficking page, is not available in China. So, anything I say has to be taken with those considerations in mind.

From what we do know, there certainly is a significant amount of sexual exploitation in China, a significant amount of forced labor, indentured servitude. There is the forced marriage issue that Congressman Smith referred to that certainly is accentuated by the one child policy. There is the issue of the North Korean refugees who come into China in large numbers, and many of them end up being trafficked into sexual exploitation, labor, or marriage. And there is an issue that does not often get talked about when you look at trafficking, and that is the trafficking of Chinese abroad to other countries. When we look at this human slavery issue, we like to look at it in both directions.

Certainly there have been cases in the United States where "snakeheads" deceived and took young Chinese who ended up in slavery in the United States. There was one big case in the New

York area years ago in garment factories, I believe, and there have been other cases. When I visit other countries, for example, Malaysia, this issue comes up, the trafficking of Chinese citizens abroad. So, China is a source country as well. Many Chinese citizens suffer abroad because of trafficking. It is an issue I tried to raise with Chinese officials.

Well, let us look at some of the positives, and then look at some of the things that need to be done. I think that you do have some awareness training going on. The ILO, whose representative is going to testify later, has been involved in this, with our support. You do have some training of officials going on. You do have a government NGO, the All-China Women's Federation, that appears, based on my visits, to have an understanding of the trafficking issue. You certainly have scholars in China with whom I met that understand the trafficking issue, and you have officials now talking more about the trafficking issue. I have engaged in dialogues in Washington, D.C., as well as in China, on this issue.

But here are some of the challenges. I think China needs to improve its anti-trafficking in persons law. The law really does not cover forced labor, and it is very narrowly defined in terms of sexual exploitation. I understand that there is an effort under way to draft such a law, and clearly that will help. There need to be shelters in places such as Yunnan province, where there are a significant number of Burmese trafficking victims. There needs to be openness about statistics. Congressman Smith referred to the large number of prosecutions and arrests that are reported. We do not know the number of convictions, and more openness would be helpful in this regard.

I think China needs to use its embassies abroad more. Visits I have paid to countries such as Malaysia tell me that China does not do as much as some of its South Asian neighbors do in terms of using their embassies abroad to provide help to victims who originate in China.

I think that another thing that must be done is to stop punishing the victims. There is evidence that victims who are found in China are punished through fines. Now, in the course of conversations in China, I had one official from the Ministry of Public Security tell me that this policy had been stopped, but then a day or two later we got contrary information, that it was still being carried on and many victims were still being punished.

I think China has to start looking at trafficking victims who originate in North Korea as trafficking victims and not as economic migrants. There is a difference. I think there are enough reports to show that this is a very significant problem.

I think it would help also if we look at the big picture. This does relate to the issue of openness. I will come back to where I started out.

If China becomes open to NGOs, if China becomes open to people from abroad meeting with its victims, if China becomes open with its statistics, if China exchanges or encourages the exchange of information on modern-day slavery, not just government official to government official, but citizen to citizen, NGO to NGO, then I think we will see some progress.

This modern-day slavery challenge is because of efforts like those of this Commission, starting to receive attention the world over. Every year for the last couple of years, we see more and more media attention to this issue. As people become aware of this issue, whether in China, the United States, or everywhere, they say, "What? Slavery in the 21st century? Let us do something about it." In the last couple of years, in part through the efforts of the Congress, the efforts of President Bush, last year we saw about 3,000 convictions of traffickers worldwide; several years ago it was in the hundreds.

Last year, we saw several hundred shelters around the world set up. Before, there were just a few score. Last year, 39 countries passed anti-trafficking in persons laws. It was just a handful when this Congress passed the law back in 2000.

So, efforts like this hearing you are holding today can bring about progress. The more we spotlight this issue, the more people all over the world want to do something to abolish slavery.

Thank you, Mr. Chairman.

[The prepared statement of Mr. Miller appears in the appendix.]

Chairman HAGEL. Ambassador Miller, thank you very much.

Let me ask my colleagues if it would be appropriate, maybe we would take a round of five minutes each on questions, if you can stay.

Mr. MILLER. Mr. Chairman, if you would allow me to have Mr. Taylor, my reports officer, join me.

Chairman HAGEL. Certainly.

Mr. MILLER. He having just come back from China, could help me with the latest information. I would appreciate it.

Chairman HAGEL. Welcome, Mr. Taylor.

Let me begin. Again, thank you, Ambassador Miller, for your good work. Please extend our appreciation to your colleagues as well.

You have covered, in general terms, a good deal of the areas of greatest concern, and in particular you mentioned strengthening the laws against forced labor in China. Then you mentioned some of the things that you felt needed to be done, that could be done in fact, to assist victims. You talked about shelters, better statistics, use of Chinese embassies abroad to help the victims, and stopping punishment of victims was one of your last points.

Let me ask this question. In light of what you have just said, do you believe that we have a good idea of the scope of the problem, of the trafficking problem in China?

Mr. MILLER. Not good enough. I would have said, two or three years ago, Senator, that we did not have a good scope of the problem in most of the world. But we are learning more and more about it. As you can tell from our report that the Secretary puts out every June, we now have more and more information. But I would say no. As I said at the beginning, with regard to China, there is much more we would like to know.

Chairman HAGEL. In your opinion, what prevents the Chinese Government from putting more law enforcement resources into the issue of trafficking, to implement and enforce their current laws, noting, as you have said, that there is some recognition of this problem. Why hasn't the Chinese Government put an appropriate number of law enforcement officials in this area?

Mr. MILLER. I do not have an exact answer for you, Mr. Chairman, because I do not know exactly how many resources they are putting in. I mean, it is not like I can tell you exactly how many dollars, and how many prosecutors, and how many police are involved in this effort. But I think my experience has been, when it comes to law enforcement in countries around the world, far more important than dollars is national will. If the people at the top want to do something and the police and prosecutors down the line get the message, then good things start to happen.

Chairman HAGEL. You mentioned the North Korean refugee issue as one of your last points. Focusing on the North Korea issue, and also all victims of trafficking in China, does the Chinese Government allow international NGOs in any effective way to address this issue and try to assist?

Mr. MILLER. Not to my knowledge. I think you will hear from Mr. Lee on this later. I think most of the work that is done, is done underground by necessity.

Chairman HAGEL. Are there any significant differences, in your opinion, in the ways that Hong Kong and Taiwan deal with these trafficking issues, as opposed to China?

Mr. MILLER. Well, Hong Kong and Taiwan, of course, are smaller areas. Taiwan has a serious challenge. We downgraded Taiwan from Tier 1 to Tier 2 last year, based on treatment of victims.

The big challenge in Hong Kong—well, there are two challenges. They have tremendous importation of domestic servants, and they also have the sex industry. From what I have learned of Hong Kong, they seem to be handling the domestic servant issue pretty well. There are very few complaints that I was able to find in Hong Kong. With regard to sex trafficking, I think Hong Kong has a bigger problem than they think they have. They believe it is non-existent. But when I talk to foreign embassies in Hong Kong, one gets a different story. So, they can improve there, as every jurisdiction can.

Mr. Taylor, did you want to add more on either Hong Kong or Taiwan?

Mr. TAYLOR. Perhaps just a note on Taiwan. There appears to be a growing trafficking problem involving young women from the Chinese mainland, crossing the Taiwan Strait without documentation, knowing that they are breaking a migration statute, but falling victim to servitude upon arrival in Taiwan. Unfortunately, given the unique nature of cross-Strait relations, there is not an easy way to protect and repatriate them responsibly.

As Ambassador Miller noted, we have tried to highlight this in the last "Trafficking in Persons Report" on both sides of the Strait, the greater responsibility that needs to be shown by Taiwan authorities to treat these women as true victims as opposed to a security threat, and also the responsibility of the PRC Government to accept these women back as victims and not punish them, fine them, and put them into a forced counseling session.

Chairman HAGEL. Thank you.

Ambassador Miller, would you like to respond to anything in particular from Congressman Smith's testimony?

Mr. MILLER. Not at all. Nothing.

Chairman HAGEL. You would, I assume, agree with Congressman Smith's assessment, as he presented it?

Mr. MILLER. Yes.

Chairman HAGEL. Mr. Taylor, anything that you would like to add?

Mr. TAYLOR. No.

Chairman HAGEL. Thank you.

Congressman Leach.

Representative LEACH. One thing that Representative Smith noted was the distinction between arrests and convictions. He noted that he did not know what the sentences are when there are convictions. Do you have any sense for that?

Mr. MILLER. We have gotten information on sentences that indicates that when sentences are given, they are tough. You can get the death penalty under Chinese law for forcing a child under 14 into prostitution, for example. But we do not know how many convictions there were and how many sentences there were. We are seeking this information through our Embassy in Beijing. We hope to have this information for this coming June's report.

Representative LEACH. You noted, and I thought quite impressively, that some 39 countries have passed anti-trafficking laws in recent years. Are there some relevant models, both of law and of enforcement, that are happening elsewhere that might apply to China?

Mr. MILLER. There are many countries that have passed these laws. In fact, there were almost 40 countries in 2004 that passed anti-trafficking legislation.

I would hesitate to cite one model. For example, we have a model law that we distribute to countries that the Department of Justice has prepared. But I always feel that a country has its own specific problems, so models are fine, but that does not mean you can—for example, Benin has just gone through an incredibly good process in drafting a law in Africa. But I do not know that you can take a law from Benin and just drop it into China. It might be worth looking at, but I would not recommend just adopting it because each country has particular trafficking problems.

Representative LEACH. Congressman Smith laid out the extraordinary dimension of the female versus male demographics in China, with the obvious implication that this will provide incentives to deepen, rather than lessen, the problem.

Does our government have any suggestions to China on this front, and are you making them?

Mr. MILLER. Well, I do not know if we have had official demarches of this nature. That is a little out of my scope. I did raise the issue when I was in Beijing, as it related to the increasing threat of trafficking. I have seen figures suggesting that the male-female ratio will be approaching a 13:10 ratio at some point. This has serious consequences. But I cannot tell you. I could find out, if you want. I cannot tell you exactly what official position the United States has taken with China on this broad issue.

Representative LEACH. Thank you very much.

Thank you, Mr. Chairman.

Chairman HAGEL. Secretary Law.

Mr. LAW. Thank you. As I mentioned in my opening statement, the Department of Labor has partnered constructively with the Chinese Government on programs and projects to improve worker protections in that country. In those instances, we found the Chinese Government to be solicitous of our help, wanting our input, and being relatively transparent on those issues.

I was interested to get a sense, Ambassador Miller, of what deliverables you have sought from the Chinese Government in this particular area, and the extent to which you feel the Chinese Government has been responsive on those issues; and to the extent they have not been forthcoming, where you think the resistance lies.

Mr. MILLER. Well, when we were in China just a month or two ago, we laid out just about every issue I raised in my statement. We laid out the issue of statistics, we laid out the issue of convictions, we laid out the issue of the North Koreans and economic migrants, we laid out the issue of the punishing of victims. What else did we lay out? That is pretty much it. I also laid out the issue of the Chinese Government using its embassies abroad to protect its own citizens.

So we are looking for progress on all of these issues. We are approaching the time of year when we get information back from our embassies and from foreign governments so we will see what has happened, and what is happening.

In terms of deliverables, at the time of my trip, the only deliverable I recall was the statement by an official at a meeting that they were going to, or had, stopped levying fines on victims. That is about it, Mark?

Mr. TAYLOR. That, and looking a little more closely at the law enforcement threat on the Burma border and trying to expand the cooperation with its neighbors. We understand cooperation with Vietnam is particularly strong and growing as the threat of Vietnamese being sold as wives is being taken seriously.

Mr. LAW. But was your sense that the response from the Chinese Government indicated that this was a priority to them, that there was some urgency attached to it, or was it simply kind of a polite response to your concerns and not much more?

Mr. MILLER. It depended on who we met with. It varied. Some were of the former category and some were of the latter category. I think it is fair to say that many of the responses involved a defensiveness. Of course, that is not unique to China. I get that defensiveness in other countries. I certainly tried to emphasize, this is the problem we all face. We face this in the United States. It is a worldwide problem. We are asking for your cooperation. A lot of attention is paid to rankings, but it is a tool to focus on the issue and help free victims and throw traffickers in jail.

Mr. LAW. All right.

One of the key issues that you mentioned in your statement is the importance of appropriately classifying different groups. For example, among those who are coming across the border from North Korea to China, some have been classified as being economic migrants, while others in that same group may be victims of human trafficking because of the element of deception or coercion that is involved. To your knowledge, is there an awareness within the Chinese Government that what we are seeing in North Korea is not merely people sneaking across the border of their own volition or being smuggled, but that there is actually a coercive element to it that needs to be addressed?

Mr. MILLER. I did not get any sense of awareness on that issue from Chinese officials. I did find some interest in the issue from the All-China Women's Federation, but beyond that, I do not recall any response. I raised this at just about every meeting I had.

I did want to add one other issue that comes up in China and elsewhere. When we talk about statistics, there is the problem of getting convictions, but also, when you look at these thousand arrests and prosecutions, one of the reasons that we need better statistics is it is hard to determine whether these are all trafficking arrests and prosecutions or whether, in China, as in many other countries, trafficking and smuggling are conflated.

Mr. LAW. Right. The terms are confused, but they are actually quite distinct because in the trafficking area there is the element of coercion or intimidation or deception. Right.

Mr. MILLER. Our office is concerned about slavery and trafficking.

Mr. LAW. Right.

Mr. MILLER. Sometimes there is confusion and countries will submit statistics—I do not know if this is the case in China—that show large numbers, and then when we look more closely, it turns out to be smuggling arrests, prosecutions, and convictions as opposed to slavery cases.

Mr. LAW. Yes. One last, quick question. This is a subject that I think, Mr. Ambassador, you and I are both familiar with in our dealings with another country.

When we talk about the issue of law enforcement, particularly when it has to do with purely internal human trafficking, very often the response we get from the national government is that this is a local law enforcement matter and something that the national government has no role in. It is as if they all discovered the 10th amendment to the U.S. Constitution. But, in fact, would you say that, because of the complicity of local law enforcement in some of these human trafficking and forced labor cases, and because there are often local cultural and economic pressures that essentially tolerate the presence of trafficking and forced labor, you really have to have a national commitment to law enforcement, even if the primary agents of that law enforcement are at the local level? Would you say that is true?

Mr. MILLER. Absolutely. I think, to some extent, China has recognized this point, as in this attention to a national law and a national plan. To that extent, to the extent they understand it is a problem, I think they understand that it is a national problem.

Mr. TAYLOR. If I could just add, in China it seems that the greatest priority is on internal trafficking, and there does seem to be considerable and expanding concern about the issue of young girls, particularly, being trafficked from places like Yunnan province up to the north to fill that gender gap that has been discussed already. That is where the law enforcement resources seem to be applied. In that sense, there is more talk and more willingness to discuss that, ironically, even though it is an internal matter, but less focus and attention on the external coming into China.

Mr. MILLER. Or going out. Yes.

Mr. LAW. Thank you so much for all your hard work and leadership on this issue.

Mr. MILLER. Thank you for your work on this trafficking issue in China, India, and other places.

Chairman HAGEL. Congressman Levin?

Representative LEVIN. Thank you.

Welcome. Nice to see you again.

Mr. MILLER. Thank you.

Representative LEVIN. Just a quick follow-up question. To the extent this is a matter of legitimate international concern, and I think it clearly is—and this relates, I suppose, to virtually every issue vis-a-vis China and the United States, or China and other countries—what is our strategy for follow-through? What are the possible avenues?

The Secretary mentioned that in China, and others also referred to this point, laws on the books do not mean very much. I do not want to use the word "leverage," perhaps, but how do we have an impact?

Mr. MILLER. All right. This is a question I ask myself every day. I think there are a number of ways. Certainly we try to directly engage the officials of the government in question. I have had discussions with Chinese Government officials here, I had discussions in Beijing. In most countries, but not in China, we engage with NGOs. We encourage NGOs.

Representative LEVIN. With China?

Mr. MILLER. Yes, with China. But I would say, in addition, it is important to know the difference. In many countries, when I visit a country, I speak out in the news media. There was a press conference in China that the U.S. Embassy organized, and there was coverage in Reuters, but I do not think it got into the Chinese newspapers.

Now, there is this report, and I do think countries are concerned, and China—I do believe China is concerned—about how they are evaluated in this report. When this report comes out, countries' governments may criticize the ratings, but I think sometimes governments may be pleased or embarrassed by the ratings, as the case may be. Certainly Chinese officials mention this report. I am trying to remember the meeting that we were at where the first 40 minutes was taken up with a denunciation of the report by the Chinese official across from me, explaining why the report was wrong. So, this is another means of engagement. Have I left out anything?

Mr. TAYLOR. Just a couple of other manifestations of the dialogue, which is relatively young, on this issue. But there is a Global Issues Forum.

Mr. MILLER. Yes. That is where I engaged in a dialogue on this issue. Last June or July, they came to Washington, D.C. There were many issues discussed, and this was one.

Mr. TAYLOR. Then there is the law enforcement dialogue that is chaired by the Assistant Secretary for International Narcotics and Law Enforcement Affairs, and we also participate in that.

Mr. MILLER. Yes.

Representative LEVIN. All right. Thank you.

Chairman HAGEL. Ambassador Miller, I have one question. It is regarding the U.N. Protocols on Trafficking and Migrant Smuggling. This is the question: why has China not signed those two U.N. protocols?

Mr. MILLER. I raised that issue and the answer was, "We are considering it." The answer was, "You considered it for a long time, we are considering it for a long time." I encouraged them to sign the U.N. Protocol. I would add that for whoever signs it, the U.N. Protocol is only as good as the will exercised by the government that signs it.

Chairman HAGEL. Thank you.

Any other questions, Mr. Secretary?

Mr. LAW. No.

Chairman HAGEL. Congressman Leach?

Representative LEACH. No.

Chairman HAGEL. Congressman Levin?

Representative LEVIN. No.

Chairman HAGEL. Thank you.

Ambassador Miller, thank you.

Mr. MILLER. Thank you.

Chairman HAGEL. Mr. Taylor, thank you.

Mr. TAYLOR. Thank you.

Chairman HAGEL. If the next panel would come forward. Thank you.

Welcome. Thank you for your time and your presentations. As you know, we have showered great accolades and recognition on each of you in our earlier introduction, so I will dispense with that and ask each of you to present your testimony. Then, if you can stay, we would very much like to engage in some questions.

So, Mr. Plant, we will begin with you. Thank you.

STATEMENT OF ROGER PLANT, HEAD, SPECIAL ACTION PROGRAM TO COMBAT FORCED LABOR, INTERNATIONAL LABOR ORGANIZATION, GENEVA, SWITZERLAND

Mr. PLANT. Thank you very much, Senator Hagel, Congressmen Leach and Levin, and Deputy Secretary Law. It is a real honor and pleasure to be with you today.

We have frequently highlighted our appreciation of the leadership displayed by the U.S. Government in national and international action against trafficking.

I have a prepared statement. I shall leave this with you and I shall just add some comments.

Chairman HAGEL. Each of your statements will be included in full in the record. Thank you.

Mr. PLANT. I have been a frequent visitor to China since its government requested ILO cooperation on forced labor and human trafficking in 2002, the same year that the activities of the ILO Special Action Program to Combat Forced Labor, which I have been privileged to head, commenced its activities.

To place these activities in their proper context, I would like to say a few words about the ILO's overall approach to human trafficking.

Last year, we launched our global report, "A Global Alliance Against Forced Labor," which gives the first estimates by an international organization of modern forced labor. A total of 12.3 million victims, of which 9.8 million are in Asia and 2.5 million are victims of trafficking; most are trafficked into commercial sexual exploitation, but at least one-third are trafficked into other forms of economic exploitation. Four out of every five cases of forced labor in the world today involve exploitation by private agents rather than by the state. Trafficking of women and children, mainly for sexual exploitation, is particularly serious, but men and boys can also be trafficked for other forms of economic exploitation.

When mainly private agents exploit forced labor victims, the offenses of trafficking, forced labor, and modern slavery are closely linked. As we heard from Deputy Secretary Law, it is precisely the coercion, usually at the end of the trafficking cycle, together with the deception that distinguishes the crime of trafficking from the crime of smuggling.

The ILO's mandate covers labor rights, the promotion of employment, the promotion of decent work. This, in its tripartite structure of governments, business employers, and workers and trade unions, gives it a unique role in action against human trafficking.

We involve labor as well as business actors, labor institutions both inside and outside government, blending law enforcement, prevention, and rehabilitation. Our approach combines activities in sender and destination countries for trafficking victims, which is a key aspect of our approach in China.

Now, Ambassador John Miller has already brought your attention to the need to focus on the trafficking and exploitation to which Chinese people can be exposed abroad. Indeed, this has been quite a large aspect of our own cooperation with China, so I will dwell to some extent on it.

As the U.S. State Department's report has recognized, and as all speakers have recognized today, there are signs of China's commitment to action against trafficking. We have seen some of the statistics on several thousand arrests and prosecutions. We know of information campaigns on the dangers of trafficking, and of increased international cooperation. But a drawback is that penal legislation covers only the trafficking of women and children.

Briefly, I would like to comment now on ILO activities. We began our activities in China in Yunnan province of China several years ago. This was part of a regional effort in the greater Mekong subregion to prevent the trafficking of women and children. A project to prevent trafficking in girls and young women, focusing in large part on labor exploitation, got under way in 2004, implemented with the All-China Women's Federation as the main partner. This addresses trafficking within China itself, focusing on three sender provinces and two destination provinces in China.

Since 2002, the ILO, largely under the aegis of our Special Action Program on Forced Labor, has cooperated with China over forced labor concerns, including trafficking. The government first sought assistance on broader forced labor concerns to prepare the ground for anticipated eventual ratification of the ILO's two Conventions on Forced Labor.

The main focus of this cooperation has been on reforms to the Reeducation Through Labor system, through technical seminars in China, and two study tours overseas, the first in 2003, the next in early 2005. An aim of this cooperation has been to strengthen a network of officials from key government agencies to advance the process of law and policy reform. It began with a focus on Reeducation Through Labor, but since 2004, trafficking has also been an important part of this cooperation.

Since September 2004, we have been implementing a U.S.-funded project on forced labor and trafficking, the role of labor institutions in law enforcement, and international cooperation in China. This project has activities in both China and several European destination countries. It includes policy advice, awareness raising, and capacity building at both central and provincial levels, activities with employers and workers' organizations against trafficking, and research and awareness raising in the destination countries.

In China, activities have concentrated on Fujian, Zhejiang, and Jilin provinces, which, as I am sure you are aware, have been the main sender provinces for Chinese workers going overseas. More recently, from the rust belt of northeastern China, Jilin, Heilongjiang, and Liaoning provinces, but increasingly so from Fujian and Zhejiang provinces in the southeast.

Our project has stimulated important debates on law and policy, notably the difference between existing Chinese approaches to trafficking and those of the Palermo Trafficking Protocol. It has enabled a review of national legislation on forced labor, trafficking and smuggling, as well as comparative studies.

In April 2005, in a workshop that I attended in Beijing, we brought key officials together to compare approaches and to seek to harmonize Chinese law and Chinese policy with emerging international standards.

I think you understand the importance of this, having heard the statements of the previous witnesses, the real importance of having a Chinese understanding of law and policy on trafficking that is consistent with the emerging international law.

Then we moved down to the provincial level. Activities involved training law enforcement officials from both public security and labor bureaus, together with recruitment agencies, tourism bureaus, labor lawyers, and others. In the second of these activities, we also involved law enforcement agents and visa officials from France and the United Kingdom as among the principal destination countries.

Our main activities to date have been, as I said, in Jilin province in the northeast, and Fujian and Zhejiang provinces in the southeast. My written statement gives far more details about what we have been doing, why we have been doing it, and what we have achieved, so I am not going to go into more detail in this oral statement.

Concurrently, we have been carrying out a significant research program in the European destination countries. Generally, as we have heard from Ambassador Miller, there has been growing awareness that Chinese migrants can be subject to highly abusive conditions of work and transportation amounting to forced labor overseas, but there has been very little systematic research.

Tragic events, like the deaths of 20 Chinese cockle pickers in the United Kingdom, early in 2004 served to bring some attention to this issue. For example, a recent report on forced labor issues in the United States estimated that half of the victims of forced labor today are ethnic Chinese.

So to fill this gap, we first issued an overview paper, which I could leave with you for the record here, then a more rigorous case study in France, now being translated into English. I am afraid that today I can only give you the French version of this study. It covers the whole cycle of recruitment and transport, as well as the living and working conditions experienced in France. It examines the complex links between the snakeheads and the employers in the Chinese ethnic enclaves, high indebtedness, together with the reprisals or threats against the migrants or family members in China as the key factors behind this severe labor exploitation. It can take between 2 and 10 years for the average Chinese clandestine migrant to pay off this debt, so it is a severe example of modern debt bondage.

This study had immense media coverage in France, and we are now following up with similar research in Italy and the United Kingdom, where some similar problems have already been identified. Our Chinese partners see such documentation as an essential ingredient of future prevention campaigns in China itself, and a film of the Chinese experience in France has recently been completed.

What about the effectiveness of what we are doing? I have been to China five times, myself. Our program officer has been spending far more time there. Just today, we are beginning one of two training workshops with Chinese employers through the Chinese Enterprise Confederation, the first in Beijing, which starts tomorrow, and the second in Hangzhou, that is a very important part of our cooperation.

But I have certainly detected a concern to grapple with the problems. There are outstanding problems, some of them severe. We have heard of a number of these from previous witnesses today.

China is a labor-abundant country, with very high unemployment, up to 5 million people in a province like Jilin, and some local governments are actively encouraging immigration as a solution to local unemployment problems.

We know that internal migrants can also be vulnerable to trafficking. There are some signs that China is taking steps to respond to these challenges. Pilot reforms to the hukou registration system, which are now being tested in certain cities, permit equal access to employment for migrant workers.

I am glad that in 2005 China ratified the ILO's Discrimination—Employment and Occupation—Convention, which will provide a further tool to seek improvement of these conditions.

Abduction and sale of women for forced marriage, and of children for adoption, remain serious problems in China. Continued efforts are needed to clamp down on these practices.

Reform to the Reeducation Through Labor system has been incorporated in the Five-Year Legislation Plan, and a draft law regarding an alternative system of community correction has been submitted to the National People's Congress. There are different approaches to this in China. It is certainly proving a difficult issue, and we know that addressing it is taking time.

To conclude, approaches to Chinese population movements must be realistic. At a recent European meeting on clandestine and illegal Chinese migration in Europe, the emphasis was mainly on border control, fraud and visa abuse, and the use of technologies such as biometrics for identifying and stamping out fraudulent practices. Yes, this is very important, but we also have to look at prevention. We have to understand that there is, in many countries, an active demand for Chinese workers. The Chinese may pay an absolute fortune to the snakeheads, landing themselves in very severe debts, and potential reprisals against themselves and their families. They may not even look at the possibilities of legal migration.

So, this is why, at our awareness raising training program in Fujian, particularly the U.K. people there insisted that there must be more understanding of how people can migrate legally in order to take the ground away from the snakeheads. So we argue that it is vital to promote safe and legal migration, and sometimes it can be fruitless to make efforts to persuade people not to move.

So what are we doing now? The first stage of our project on law enforcement, for which we gratefully acknowledge the support of the U.S. State Department, is coming to an end. But we are planning now a follow-up phase. This will have activities at both national and provincial levels.

The measures to help strengthen the law and policy framework, which you have all seen as so important, will focus on the forced labor dimensions and on trafficking for labor exploitation. Other aspects will focus on the training of provincial government officials on labor migration management, including the management of private recruitment agencies. Time and time again, we have seen that the existence of illegal employment agencies can be a large part of the problem.

We now plan to target more intensively the sender provinces of Fujian and Zhejiang, with an awareness raising program drawing on diverse tools, including hot-lines, local media, Web sites of recruitment agencies, and this will focus in particular on identified regions at high risk for potential migrants.

Finally, the dialogue between China and the destination countries has to focus on the means to prevent, as well as to combat, human trafficking. As ILO, we see a need to involve business and labor actors in this international cooperation, so we now have plans for a fairly significant meeting, which is bringing together labor institutions and authorities, law enforcement agencies, and academic experts from both sides, the destination countries, and also China, and we very much hope that such an initiative will also be of interest to the United States.

Thank you very much for your attention.

[The prepared statement of Mr. Plant appears in the appendix.]

Chairman HAGEL. Mr. Plant, thank you. I understand you flew in from Geneva for this hearing, so we are particularly grateful for your efforts to get here.

Mr. PLANT. Thank you.

Chairman HAGEL. Thank you very much.

Ms. Perkins.

STATEMENT OF WENCHI YU PERKINS, DIRECTOR, ANTI-TRAFFICKING AND HUMAN RIGHTS PROGRAM, VITAL VOICES, WASHINGTON, DC

Ms. PERKINS. Thank you. Senator Hagel, Representatives Leach, Levin, and also Deputy Secretary Law, Ambassador Miller, thank you for having today's hearing focusing on human trafficking in China. On behalf of Vital Voices Global Partnership, I just want to thank you again for focusing on this issue. Human trafficking, as Ambassador Miller said, is one of the most egregious violations of human rights in the 21st century, and no country is immune, including China.

Vital Voices has been at the forefront of anti-trafficking efforts since the mid-1990s. Our leadership was instrumental in the creation of the U.N. Anti-Trafficking Protocol and the passage of the U.S. anti-trafficking legislation in 2000.

Today, through partnerships with many outstanding NGO leaders, we continue to make positive impacts in East Asia by promoting government and civil society collaboration to counter trafficking.

I am here to share with you my personal experience encountering trafficking victims from the People's Republic of China, and also information that my organization has collected from our partners in China. My perspectives will be focused on women and children.

In my written statement, I have detailed two stories of trafficking victims whom I encountered in Chicago, Illinois. One of them was a woman who considered herself as the worst class in Chinese society, and has no future in China. She was enticed by a "snakehead," the Chinese term for human smuggler, to come to the United States. Unfortunately, she was exploited and forced to provide sexual services in a massage parlor. Threatened by her boss for deportation back to China and terrified that her family in China would be harmed because she would not be able to pay off her debts for coming into the United States, she was forced to continue working in exploited conditions.

The other story is of a teenaged boy, desperate to leave China from Fujian province because he was forced to stop formal education when he was 13 as a result of his family's violating the one child policy. He was lured into coming to the United States, was told that he could continue his education and have a better life. Unfortunately, he was exploited in the process and forced to work illegally as a forced child laborer in this country. Every time he talked to his mother, his mother mentioned that the trafficker who had arranged for his travel was harassing her on a daily basis. Therefore he was desperate to make money to pay off the debts so his mother could avoid continued harassment from the snakehead.

I am sharing with you these two stories because they are two examples of many more Chinese victims of trafficking in the United States, people who have no other options, and who have been taken advantage of and grossly exploited. They are either in debt bondage and fear for their family's safety back home, or are terrified of the snakeheads, who are often linked to organized crime syndicates.

I have witnessed a child meticulously saving every single dollar she was given by the U.S. Immigration authorities and sending them back home to her mother, because she said, "Every dollar can help my mother pay off the debts to the snakeheads so she would not be threatened by the snakeheads any more."

Most of the trafficking victims, many of them minors, are manipulated by the traffickers through the threat of deportation. They fear deportation back to China because the government punishes those who leave the country without government permission by putting them in jail. The length of the jail time depends on how much money they can raise for a bribe.

I was told by a child that those deported back to China without money for a bribe are stripped of clothes and beaten in jail. The desperation, exploitation, and inability to leave the situation makes those Chinese people, many of them women and minors, victims of human trafficking. Chinese victims are not only shipped and traded from China to more affluent countries for exploitation, many of them are also trafficked internally for forced marriage or sexual and labor exploitation, about which Congressman Smith, Ambassador Miller, and also Mr. Plant have stated. Within China, women are abducted and taken to rural areas for purchase by older men or by those who are of a low position in society and have difficulty finding a willing partner. This practice is tolerated in some less-developed areas because some Chinese even think that forced marriage is a way to prevent rape and sexual assault, since it assures that the sexual needs of these men are being met. It is also believed that the recent increase of trafficking for forced marriage is due to the imbalance in the numbers of women to men as a result of the one child policy.

Another human trafficking practice within China that has not received enough attention is trafficking for forced labor. I am glad that Mr. Plant just stated this point very well in his statement. Migrant worker issues in China have drawn world attention, as the abundance of cheap Chinese labor has made the country the world's largest sweat shop. Seventy percent of the migrant workers are females under the age of 25 who move from rural areas to the country's more prosperous south. They were told that jobs in the south could help them make the minimum wage and they would be protected by China's labor laws. In reality, forced labor over time is the norm. The factories illegally deduct meal and dormitory fees from a worker's pay. Some of them are only allowed to use the bathroom twice a day. They are literally kept as slaves.

China's migrant labor exploitation has been discussed widely, and I am grateful that the Commission has held hearings and roundtables on this subject before. However, human trafficking is more than just labor exploitation. Trafficking victims are in indentured servitude, debt bondage, unable to leave because of the potential danger they may face, or serious consequences that may ensue.

Last November, a migrant woman worker passed away in a factory in Guangdong province after being forced to work for 24 hours non-stop. Imagine what kind of pressure and control she must have faced to work herself to death. I urge the Commission and the State Department's Office to Monitor and Combat Trafficking in Persons to pay special attention to this form of human trafficking.

Trafficking into China is gradually gaining more attention with the North Korean refugees being exploited in China. I know that my colleague will provide more detailed information later, so I will not cover this in my oral statement.

The Chinese Government is paying attention to human trafficking, and actively cracks down on trafficking cases. Some prevention pilot projects and temporary shelters for trafficking victims into China do exist. However, they are limited to certain regions. The government effort to protect and rehabilitate returned trafficking victims is insufficient to address the problem.

The U.S. Congress plays a vital role to help address the modern-day slavery from, within, and into China. In my written statement, I have six recommendations, and I will point out a few here.

The U.S. Congress should make greater resources available to promote collaboration between government and NGOs in China. There are more than a few independent NGOs and research institutes in China that can complement government efforts, while providing professional services and making positive changes.

The Chinese Government recognizes that this is a serious problem and that they need civil society to assist in its counter-trafficking work. Therefore, civil society capacity building and leadership training for NGO leaders is the key to successful government and civil society collaboration.

The Commission should analyze the various forms of trafficking, especially those under-addressed issues of trafficking from the East Coast, or for forced labor, and trafficking for forced labor exploitation internally. Then the Congress should authorize funding to support large-scale awareness-raising campaigns to prevent human trafficking, targeting at-risk populations and areas such as Yunnan, Guangxi, Fujian, Hunan, Gansu, Zhejiang, and Jilin provinces.

The Congress and the U.S. Government should call on the international business community to help change and prevent the practices of exploiting migrant labor. The business sector can complement the Chinese Government's and NGOs' anti-trafficking efforts. Many garment, toy, and other labor-intensive factories are contractors or subcontractors of international brands. Most international companies can work with their contractors in China to ensure that migrant workers are not exploited, and that employers abide by China's labor laws.

Last, I want to thank the Commission again for bringing this issue to everyone's attention. Human trafficking is a complex issue that requires a comprehensive and multi-stakeholder approach.

China is the most populous country and one of the most powerful emerging markets in the world. We must start working with the government and civil society in China to address this growing global challenge.

Thank you.

[The prepared statement of Ms. Perkins appears in the appendix.]

Chairman HAGEL. Ms. Perkins, thank you very much.

Mr. Lee.

STATEMENT OF ABRAHAM LEE, DIRECTOR OF PUBLIC RELATIONS, CROSSING BORDERS, COLLEGE PARK, MD

Mr. LEE. Thank you. Senator Hagel, Congressman Leach, Members of the Congressional-Executive Commission on China, on behalf of the staff at Crossing Borders, I thank you for the privilege of testifying before this Commission and for the opportunity to give voice to the thousands of North Korean refugees still suffering in China. We at Crossing Borders are a group of Korean and Chinese Americans who feel passionately about the situation of North Koreans in Northeast China.

Since 2003, we have maintained a continuing presence in the field and have been at the front lines of providing assistance and care to these refugees. It is our field team of U.S.-based staff and local Chinese staff, actively working along the border, that gives us a unique glimpse into the current situation in China.

As has been widely reported, the widespread famine of the late 1990s created a mass exodus of North Korean refugees into China. Starvation drove refugees to search desperately for food and survival across the icy rivers and snowy mountains that line the North Korean/Chinese border. Nearly 10 years later, North Koreans still suffer from hunger and still risk everything to cross into China. They are in search of food, clothing, medicine, shelter, and possibly a better life.

Human traffickers stand as an ominous threat to their freedom and well-being. In a project called Road to Refuge, we traced the path a refugee might take in escaping to China. Through the wilderness and mountains, refugees hide in ditches along the road to avoid being caught by traffickers, who, with their barking dogs, set up at look-outs along the commonly used path.

As a 15-year-old, a young girl named So-Young and a friend crossed the river, entered into China, and immediately were approached by Chinese men who offered them work at 300 renminbi per month, approximately US $36. Thinking they were too young to be sold as a wife or slave, they were enticed to follow these men. So-Young awoke the following morning alone, her friend sold to a Chinese buyer. Her captors forced her to work until she grew taller and could be sold as well. The first potential buyer was a 40-year-old man in search of a wife. She refused, and continued to stubbornly refuse attempts to sell her. Knowing her protests would soon go ignored and result in her forced sale to a Chinese man, she enlisted the help of a deacon in a local underground church who had secretly ministered to her in the village. She lived three years as a refugee in hiding, until she was captured, repatriated to North Korea, and spent six months in prison.

Escaping to China a second time, she was caught by traffickers again, and this time was raped by her sellers. She was then sold to a Chinese man, who also raped her multiple times before she was able to run away.

Today, she lives in one of our shelters and faces, daily, the possibility of being captured again. She says, "There are many people coming out of North Korea, but they do not have anywhere to go, and no other choice but to go that route into China."

Unfortunately, stories like hers are all too common. As long as the Chinese Government does little to fight human trafficking, women will continue to be susceptible to the forced sex trade to satisfy the growing number of Chinese men who, because of poor economic and social status, cannot find a wife of their own.

Even if a refugee is able to avoid the snare of human traffickers, they still face the daily hostility of Chinese authorities and secret North Korean agents in China.

In recent years, China has grown exponentially, economically, and secured a prominent place on the world stage. Yet, the Chinese Government continues to flagrantly disregard their obligations under international agreements and stand uncontested as they actively hunt down North Koreans and send them back to face imprisonment, torture, and possibly execution.

Their actions jeopardize the lives of North Koreans and the workers who struggle valiantly to render them assistance. Last December, we were forced to shut down one of our shelters because of this kind of Chinese persecution. We were forced to cease helping two North Korean teenagers, and another teenager was captured trying to escape to South Korea, and likely has been repatriated back to North Korea. Our local administrator, a Chinese citizen facing harsh punishment from Chinese authorities if caught, was forced to go into hiding, leaving behind his family for approximately one month.

The work of helping North Koreans is not without its stories of hope and success as well. We are encouraged by the children in our ministry who represent hope for a Nation and its people. Unfortunately, these stories are not as common as we would like. The Chinese Government must be forced to abide by its obligations as signatories to the 1951 Convention Relating to the Status of Refugees and its 1967 Protocol. Under the agreement, many North Koreans have a legitimate right to be in China, and China has an obligation to accommodate them.

Non-governmental organizations must be granted free access to these refugees. Failure to do so creates an atmosphere of lawlessness, where human traffickers work virtually unimpeded. Chinese Government pressure forces humanitarian workers to work in secret and severely limits the scope of help we are able to give. There are thousands of refugees in hiding in China; only a small fraction are able to receive aid.

In conclusion, I thank you again for this opportunity to testify before this Commission, which is in a unique position to shape the United States' policy toward China. We pray that, through the combined efforts of the United States and humanitarian workers from around the world, that relief would come to the thousands of suffering North Koreans in China.

Thank you.

[The prepared statement of Mr. Lee appears in the appendix.]

Chairman HAGEL. Mr. Lee, thank you.

To each of you, once again, thank you for your testimony.

Mr. Plant, let me begin with you. You noted toward the end of your testimony that the ILO's efforts to involve more groups in the trafficking issue included, I think you used the term, "business actors."

Could you tell this Commission a little more about how you are recruiting businesses, business leaders, to this effort?

Mr. PLANT. Thank you, Senator, for a very important question. If you do not mind, I will digress for a few seconds and talk more globally before coming back to China. I am glad to say that, at the end of January, a meeting was held in Athens, at which CEOs and influential business leaders signed themselves up to a global campaign to involve business against trafficking.

We are a tripartite organization, so of course we try to harness employers' organizations to our efforts. I was very glad to attend and make an opening statement of that meeting. We will be having a follow-up meeting in Geneva this coming Saturday at which some influential business leaders will be trying to get 1,000 major companies to sign up to these ethical principles.

Now I shall turn to China. We have had a number of discussions and ongoing dialogue with our principal partner, the Chinese Enterprise Confederation [CEC], and we agreed that we would host two meetings this week. I was hoping to be there, but was persuaded to come here and have my colleague organize these meetings. This will be part of our activities to make Chinese companies and business leaders, including those who are involved in the export sector, aware of the realities of what is forced labor, and how they can identify it and how they can prevent its occurrence at the enterprise level. We see this awareness as a key part of our overall activities to prevent forced labor and trafficking in China, but it is part of a global effort of the ILO, which has now committed itself to seeking the eradication of all forms of forced labor worldwide by 2015.

Chairman HAGEL. Thank you. We are grateful for your efforts to include these groups, and particularly the business groups, because, as you have noted, and I think most of us understand, that this is a group of individuals that can bring tremendous resources and leadership to this effort, and I suspect have been left out to some extent over the years. We have focused on governments and NGOs, primarily. So, anything I can do, or this Commission can do, to assist you in that effort with the business community, please let us know.

Mr. PLANT. Thank you very much.

Chairman HAGEL. Thank you.

Ms. Perkins, Mr. Lee, let me ask each of you, what is your evaluation of the Chinese Government's relationship with NGOs in China, specifically in the area of trafficking?

Ms. PERKINS. Thank you, Senator Hagel. It is our understanding that the All China Women's Federation, established as a non-governmental organization, but influenced by the Chinese Government, provides legal assistance to victims of trafficking. Although they are not seen as an independent non-governmental organization, they do provide services available to trafficking victims. In addition, they partner with international government organizations, such as UNICEF, to provide all kinds of pilot projects to prevent trafficking of human beings, especially in Guangxi province.

As for independent, non-governmental organizations, Vital Voices has several partners in China that are attached to academic institutes as non-governmental organizations and research institutes. Even though they are attached to national universities, their work is considered independent. Some of them provide legal assistance to victims of forced marriage.

So, I would say there are creative ways to work with organizations and institutions such as those to promote anti-trafficking efforts, rather than establishing the provocative NGOs that we are thinking about in China, which the Chinese authorities might see more as a challenge to their power.

Chairman HAGEL. Thank you.

Mr. Lee.

Mr. LEE. With regard to Chinese NGOs, I cannot speak intelligently on that. But with regard to the work of Crossing Borders and the few NGOs that are working in Northeast China to help North Korean refugees, I can tell you that we have no relationship with the Chinese Government. As a matter of fact, we have an antagonistic relationship in which, if we were to be discovered, we would likely be imprisoned and subsequently deported. So, all of the work that we do is clandestine in nature and is not public.

Chairman HAGEL. Thank you, Mr. LEE.

Congressman Leach.

Representative LEACH. One of the dilemmas that this Commission has, and the U.S. Government has, is that one has the sense that almost anything that is critical of China is almost counter-productive today. In the history of human rights, U.S. Government advocacy has generally been a little bit helpful in many parts of the world. But one has the sense now, if a U.S. Government official comes in and says something, the Chinese will think the reverse. So one of the dilemmas becomes answering the question, "What is the most constructive way to act?" Now having said that, our American society is rooted in clarity of convictions, and we can never back off our convictions. But we also have to deal with things realistically. So, one of the things in foreign affairs that the United States does in many countries, for other reasons, some of which relate to corruption problems, is that we assist nonprofits, non-governmental organizations. Even though there are some sensitivities that have arisen in recent years, we have largely been a supporter of international organizations such as the ILO. So there are other techniques than simply the U.S. Government sponsoring a program.

Are there institutions of Chinese governance that have responded positively in the last four or five years? Are there governmental institutions, the analogue to attorneys general, in provinces or local police that we ought to be assisting where they do things right, instead of simply pointing out where there are great gaps in the system? Do you know of anything of this nature? Ms. Perkins, perhaps you would be able to respond.

Ms. PERKINS. According to our partners, we have learned that within the Chinese central government, there used to be a bureau dedicated to anti-trafficking work. But as a result of the Chinese Government's streamlining policy, I think that office no longer exists. However, I read that there are intergovernmental agencies or a working committee working on anti-trafficking issues.

I think I want to bring everyone's attention to the issue that the Chinese term "trafficking" is actually seen as "abduction and selling"—*gui mai*. The concept of trafficking, defined by international law, is slightly different from that which exists in China. I think it is very important that, while the Chinese Government is actively cracking down on trafficking cases, most of those cases are abductions and selling of human beings.

The question is how to bring the national Chinese definition of trafficking in compliance with the international definition, which has a much broader definition, and also covers cases of trafficking for forced labor and exploitation of migrant workers. I think that is worth our attention.

Representative LEACH. Mr. Plant, would you care to respond?

Mr. PLANT. Thank you very much, Congressman Leach. I have to go all over the world, working with governments in sometimes difficult situations. There is no question that there can be sensitivities over the wider issue of forced labor, and also trafficking in persons. I think what Ms. Perkins has said is very important. Several witnesses have repeated this discrepancy over definitions. What I would like to say is that we, as the ILO, since we have engaged with the Government of China, have a very positive relationship with this group of partners in the National People's Congress, in the State Council, the Ministry of Labor, the Ministry of Justice, and the Ministry of Public Security, first at a national level, then, as I explained, going down to very practical cooperation at the provincial, and also lower levels. So, yes, there are some very intense discussions over concepts, but I think it is important to mention once again, which Ambassador Miller has already mentioned, that there is a draft national action plan against trafficking between 2005 and 2010, which is now being actively discussed, and it does provide for a coordinating body for anti-trafficking activity. It is a proposal. So, I think we should not underestimate the extent to which some very positive thinking is going on at various branches of both the national government and provincial governments as to how they can intensify action against trafficking. I think the focus has been almost exclusively so far on cracking down. What we are now working on with many counterparts in China is the scope for having a wider approach to trafficking, which the ILO does in every country, combining law enforcement, victim identification, prevention, rehabilitation, et cetera. I remain optimistic that progress is being made.

Representative LEACH. Let me ask, and maybe Mr. Lee and Ms. Perkins in particular, is there a widespread Chinese social understanding of the issue? That is, is this something that the typical Chinese citizen is, (a) very aware of, and (b) very concerned about?

Or is this one of these issues that is considered something people just kind of let go? Do you have any sense of that? I mean, for example, is your work welcomed by the typical Chinese citizen or is it considered an intrusion?

Mr. LEE. Well, I can only speak intelligently about Northeast China. In terms of the presence of North Koreans in China, it is certainly an issue that is well-known to those in Jilin Province and in the Yanbian Autonomous Prefecture region, and certainly along the borders. However, I do not believe that the trafficking issue is well known, and in my experiences people do not care. North Koreans are seen more as a nuisance than anything else. Even ethnically Korean Chinese citizens refuse to offer them aid. The only segment of the population, in my experience, that is actively taking a concern for these refugees is the local church and evangelical Christians in China.

Representative LEACH. Ms. Perkins.

Ms. PERKINS. I read People's Daily often, and I often read in the Chinese-language version that there are always new stories about anti-trafficking work by the government, especially those regarding trafficking for forced marriage, and also trafficking internally and externally from abduction of Vietnamese women and Burmese women into China as wives. So, I would say that, to a certain extent, I think the Chinese people do understand trafficking in that context, forced marriage, abduction of babies. However, as I said, in a broader understanding of human trafficking, I think there is very little awareness, especially in Fujian and Guangdong provinces, about the danger of migration in terms of the danger they may face in the migration process.

I was told by a former trafficking victim that before he attempted to come to the United States, in his dream the United States was paved with gold. All they fantasize about is that it is better if you get out of the country. They do not realize the exploitation and the potential danger in the migration process. Half of the citizens in the city of Fuzhou have chosen to migrate out of that city. What is wrong with that? I think it is really the low awareness about the potential danger that they may face when they choose to migrate. I think that issue needs a series of large-scale public awareness campaigns about the potential danger of human trafficking, rather than permitting people to fantasize about life overseas as a much better choice.

Representative LEACH. Thank you.

Did you want to add anything, Mr. Plant?

Mr. PLANT. I was at a seminar in Fuzhou involving all kinds of officials and recruitment agencies from these two provinces. Yes. They identified exactly what Ms. Perkins has just said, which is why we are now planning this intensive awareness-raising campaign in high-risk regions. So, yes, I agree.

Representative LEACH. Mr. Chairman, let me just conclude. What Mr. Plant, representing the ILO, has just said is one of the reasons why the United States ought to be supportive of the ILO and the institution he represents, the United Nations. Thank you.

Chairman HAGEL. Mr. Leach, I agree with your observation. We should be. Thank you, each of you.

Secretary Law.

Mr. LAW. Just one last question, following up on the very important discussion that was triggered by Mr. Leach's first question, focusing on how we find points of constructive engagement with Chinese officials where we can advance our principles without creating a direct confrontation that would end the cooperation that we need to have from Chinese authorities to advance those principles.

I thought, in particular, Mr. Plant's observations were helpful in that regard, in terms of the areas that you have been able to find where we have been able to identify common goals and interests and pursue those.

One of the areas that you mentioned—where we have not achieved the progress that we would like—is in creating a comprehensive, reliable data set that helps us understand the scope of the problem, where it lies, and therefore enables us to go after it and hold ourselves accountable for our progress in dealing with it.

I was wondering, for each of the witnesses starting with Mr. Plant, how we can create that reliable data that helps us understand the scope of human trafficking, both internally, entirely within the borders of China, as well as externally. We need to get a firmer grasp of both the in-migration, for example, from North Korea that Mr. Lee talked about, and the out-migration, for example, to the United States for trafficking purposes that Ms. Perkins talked about.

I will start with you, Mr. Plant.

Mr. PLANT. Thank you very much, Mr. Law. It is actually an extremely difficult question and one to which we have been giving a lot of attention. But ever since the ILO came up with its global estimates on forced labor and trafficking, we have been thinking, "How can we enhance national capacities to have much more reliable data, which is a prerequisite for effective action in every country, whether a sender or receiving country, or whether sending or receiving provinces within one country?" We have embarked on some significant research, as I said. It has not always been easy, even to persuade the European countries that they want to do this. But I think they have now come around to cooperating with our research. I think more research, even in this country, is needed. There are some basic estimates out there, but it is clear that much more systematic case research needs to be done.

While some of the witnesses were talking, I looked, briefly, through a research paper that has been done by one of our Chinese consultants. There is quite a lot out there. They have broken down the number of prosecutions, the kinds of issues, in three provinces. Ms. Perkins pronounces them much better than I do. I will say Fujian, Zhejiang, and Jilin. So, it is there.

But, yes, there is need for much more of this. As we have all been saying, and as all the other witnesses have been saying, until you have got some common understanding as to what is covered by the offense of trafficking, it is going to be impossible to move forward with more precise data collection. So, the conceptual issues have to go hand in hand with the data gathering and the research in order to move forward. Thank you.

Mr. LAW. All right. Thank you.

Ms. Perkins.

Ms. PERKINS. I almost wonder if we should put that much focus on compiling data. As I understand it, numbers are very important for us to understand the extent and the scope of the challenge. However, I think this issue has been around for a long time. I wonder if we should put more efforts and resources into, for example, training of judges and law enforcement to help identify victims of trafficking in China, and also putting more resources to organizations like the All-China Women's Federation. As they are sort of the semi-governmental organization, they do have some independence and they can help promote some kind of anti-trafficking efforts, especially at the provincial level.

China is a huge country. I do not think everything can be conducted through the central government. The provinces have a lot of autonomy. In reality, the province of Guangxi has been doing and piloting some of the really creative anti-trafficking projects, in coordination with other U.N. agencies. I think that kind of practice needs to be replicated by other provinces and promoted by the central government.

Mr. LAW. Thank you.

Mr. Lee.

Mr. LEE. We, as an organization, every time we take in refugees, do our best to collect as much data as possible. However, conservative estimates put the number at, I believe, 200,000 to 300,000 North Korean refugees in China. We have access to maybe 1,000 of those. So, we can collect data, and we do our best to collect data that may be representative of the entire population. However, as I have shared with you, the refugees are in hiding. You are not going to find them. It is going to be difficult to garner testimony from them, or information. In addition, I have a hard time believing that anything could be done through the central government, or even the provincial governments. It jeopardizes the lives of these North Koreans, who admittedly, when you meet with them, are highly skeptical of any visitors, particularly foreigners and Chinese officials. So I have a hard time believing that reliable data can be collected on a large scale. If it were to be done, I believe it would have to be done by independent NGOs and be sort of representative, like I said, of the entire population of refugees.

Mr. LAW. Thank you. I appreciate that.

Just briefly, with respect to the comment raised by Ms. Perkins, I could not agree more that our first priority needs to be to focus on the victims themselves and on rescuing them and providing the essential services that they need. But I would also say that it is not one or the other. It really needs to be a "both-and" effort, because I think we have even found in our own government that that which gets measured gets done, gets worked on, and gets improved.

So taking into account your very good comments—that the data is probably not completely reliable or completely comprehensive—nevertheless, it is important to develop better and more specific data to be able to have some sense of the scope of the problem. This helps put the attention that is necessary on the issue and helps us hold ourselves accountable, as well as the Chinese Government and others accountable, for achieving progress on it. But thank you for your responses.

Chairman HAGEL. Congressman Leach, any last-minute questions?

Representative LEACH. No, sir. I just want to thank the three panelists. We appreciate your perspective.

Chairman HAGEL. Secretary Law?

Mr. LAW. I do, as well. I extend my appreciation to you and to your staff for organizing this very important and informative hearing.

Chairman HAGEL. To each of our panelists, thank you for your excellent testimony. You have contributed greatly today. We obviously will be back in touch with you on some follow-up issues and some of your suggestions.

Ambassador Miller, Mr. Taylor, thank you for what you continue to do.

I might add that one of our Commissioners, Senator Brownback, has asked that a written statement be included in the record, which, without objection, it will be.

[The prepared statement of Senator Brownback appears in the appendix.]

Chairman HAGEL. Hearing adjourned.

[Whereupon, at 4:05 p.m., the hearing was concluded.]

APPENDIX

Prepared Statements

Prepared Statement of Hon. Christopher H. Smith

March 6, 2006

Thank you for holding this hearing today about the tragedy of human trafficking in China. Trafficking—the forcible exploitation for sex or labor of women, men and children—is one of the world's most serious and widespread human rights problems. It is slavery, and it is the denial of the very humanity of its victims. Sadly, human rights in China today are violated with impunity.

Since 1979, the People's Republic of China has imposed and implemented a cruel policy that has systematically rendered children illegal and dead unless authorized by a "birth allowance" certificate. The one child per couple policy imposes ruinous fines—up to 10 times both husband and wife's salary—for a child conceived outside of the government plan. As a direct result of these ongoing crimes against humanity, China today is missing millions of girls, girls who were murdered simply because they are girls. A couple of years ago, the State Department suggested that as many as 100 million girls of all ages are missing—that is to say they should be alive and well but are not, a consequence of the one child government policy. China is the only country in the world whose systematic human rights abuses touch every family without exception. It results in the mass killing of people based on their gender. Gendercide in fact constitutes one of humanity's worst blights.

Two weeks ago the Subcommittee on Africa, Global Human Rights, and International Operations, which I chair, held a hearing on the Internet in China. At the hearing, we learned that the Chinese people have little access to uncensored information about any political or human rights topic, including information about China's intentionally coercive one-child policy and its devastating contribution to the growing problem of human trafficking. This is because totalitarian regimes are propped up by two essential pillars: the secret police and propaganda. The Chinese government maintains control of its people by limiting what they know and through brute force—both systematic abuses of human rights.

Even more disturbing, U.S. technology and know-how is being used by repressive regimes in China and elsewhere in the world to cruelly exploit and abuse the citizens of those countries. While the Internet has opened up commercial opportunities and provided people all over the world with access to vast amounts of information, in China it has also become a malicious tool—a cyber-sledgehammer of repression in the hands of the government. That is why I have introduced legislation, H.R. 4780, the Global Online Freedom Act of 2006, which works to promote freedom of information on the Internet by establishing minimum corporate standards for online freedom and prohibiting U.S. businesses from hosting an e-mail server or search engine within countries that systematically restrict Internet freedom.

This hearing is particularly timely. BBC reports from January 2006 indicate that China may replace Thailand in the next few years as the region's trafficking hub, all at a time when the age of victims being trafficked is falling. With too much frequency we read news accounts of women and girls who are abducted in places like Burma, North Korea, and Vietnam and are trafficked and sold into slavery in China.

With more than one billion people in China, one must ask why there are so many women and girls being trafficked into China. After more than 25 years of coercive family planning, sex-selective abortions, infanticide, and the selling off of girl babies, there are more than 100 million missing girls. And in 2004, the most recent year for which we have statistics, 9,000 women and children were kidnapped in China. I have met with numerous victims both in China and at hearings I have chaired who have told me their horrific stories of being forced to submit to the abortion of their children. Those stories help to explain why, according to a recent State Department Human Rights Report, one consequence of China's so-called "birth limitation policies" is that 56 percent of the world's female suicides occur in China. This is five times the world average and amounts to approximately 500 suicides by women per day.

The country's male-female sex ratio is now dangerously skewed. The 2000 census revealed that there were nearly 19 million boys more than girls in the 0–15 age group. This dangerous imbalance is fueling the trafficking of women and girls as well as the sale of babies. The Chinese government must do more than pay lip service to prevent trafficking; it must immediately end its barbaric one-child policy.

Another vitally important aspect of the trafficking problem is the repression and brutal treatment of the North Korean people that brings a flood of refugees to China. Women and children are increasingly the majority of refugees crossing the river into China, many of whom are abducted by ethnic Korean Chinese traffickers who sell them either to men as wives, concubines or prostitutes. Their price and destination are often determined by their age and appearance. Tragically, kidnapping and trafficking have become common ways that Chinese men acquire women. The serious imbalances in the male-female sex ratio at birth in China make purchasing a bride attractive. Once the women or girls are sold, they are subjected to forced marriage and rape. Some accept their fate; others struggle and are punished. In violation of the United Nations Refugee Convention, to which China is a state party, China arrests and returns North Korean refugees to North Korea where they face certain imprisonment and/or execution.

Last October, I chaired a hearing on the horrific problem of North Koreans trafficked in China. Mrs. Kyeong-Sook CHA, told us how the Food Distribution Center in Pyongyang stopped distributing food at the end of June 1995. In October 1997 she jumped into Tumen River to find her daughter who had gone to China looking for food. Much later, she found out all Chinese living close to the border were involved in human trafficking. They bought and sold North Korean girls with the help of North Koreans. Mrs. Cha was hired as a maid in Hwa Ryong City along with several other North Korean women who were regularly raped. Another man bought her daughter for 4,000 Yuan (about $400), and they worked for him as servants at his house. They escaped again, but were eventually were kidnapped by human traffickers two months later. Eventually Mrs. Cha and her daughter were sent by the Chinese police to a North Korean detention center, where she found out her second daughter had also been trafficked. Mrs. Cha and her three children finally found her way to South Korea in June 2003.

Trafficking victims in China are not only from North Korea. Last year according to the Chinese Xinhua News Agency, the number of known cases of women and girls trafficked from Vietnam to China doubled. One hundred twenty-five cases of Vietnamese trafficked into China's Guangxi (guong-shee) province alone were detected, and these numbers represent only the cases reported; we do not know the stories of countless others trapped in the tragedy of trafficking.

The crime of trafficking does not affect solely women and children either. Chinese men have been trafficked for forced labor to Europe, South America, and the Middle East. A large number of Chinese men and women are smuggled abroad at enormous personal financial cost and, upon arrival in the destination country, are subjected to cruel sexual exploitation and slave labor to repay their debts.

Any serious discussion of trafficking in China must examine why thousands are trafficked every year outside China's borders despite its government's alleged commitment to eliminate the scourge of trafficking. According to reports from Harry Wu of the Laogai Research Foundation, Chinese men and women pay a fee of about $2,000 to traffickers, who with Chinese police escort, are taken to ports where they board fishing vessels destined for American shores. The ability of the traffickers to take as many as 250 people at a time out of sea ports rests on the traffickers' ability to bribe the police to allow them unhindered movement. Once in America, or other destinations, the victims are forced to work for years to pay an estimated $25,000 to $50,000. It is clear that without the assistance of the Chinese authorities, traffickers could not easily send their victims abroad.

Chinese gangs traditionally involved in prostitution in the United States are now bringing people here from China to work as laborers or prostitutes. The traffickers are notorious for their brutal treatment of victims who cannot come up with the money for payment. Their tactics include ransom, extortion, repeated rapes, and torture. Often, traffickers will only transport people with family ties so that their victims can be held hostage if payment isn't forthcoming or the victim is uncooperative.

We must loudly condemn the horrific practices which continue in China that literally and psychologically destroy human life and spirit. By way of illustration, Mrs. Gao Xiao Duan, a former administrator of a Chinese Planned Birth Control Office, testified before my Subcommittee in 1998 about China's policies. She explained, "Once I found a woman who was nine months pregnant, but did not have a birth-allowed certificate. According to the policy, she was forced to undergo an abortion surgery. In the operation room I saw how the aborted child's lips were sucking, how its limbs were stretching. A physician injected poison into its skull, and the child died, and it was thrown into the trash can. . . . I was a monster in the daytime, injuring others by the Chinese communist authorities' barbaric planned-birth policy, but in the evening, I was like all other women and mothers, enjoying my life with my children. . . . to all those injured women, to all those children who were killed, I want to repent and say sincerely that I'm sorry!"

Abortion and trafficking are the twin tragedies under which China is staggering. William Maddox, in a USA Today December 2004 article entitled "China's 'daughter dearth,'" but which could apply equally well to China's trafficking scourge, calls China's one-child policy a "humanitarian tragedy that is robbing its people one family at a time," and laments that "hundreds of millions of Chinese men will never experience the unique pleasures . . . (of being) the father of a daughter." He concludes, ". . . while I know that America can hardly stand in judgment of China's policies, somehow still I wish the Chinese could love their daughters, too." It is also my fervent wish that China will end its daughter-hating policies, restoring life and dignity to its people.

Thank you, Mr. Chairman, again for the opportunity of testifying today before the Commission about this vitally important issue.

PREPARED STATEMENT OF HON. JOHN R. MILLER

MARCH 6, 2006

Thank you for the opportunity to address this important subject.

Trafficking in persons is modern-day slavery, a global phenomenon that affects human rights, public health and international security.

Human traffickers today use kidnapping, fraud, psychological abuse and beatings to force men, women and children into labor and sex exploitation.

Today's forms of slavery extend into every country in the world, including the United States. The "Trafficking in Persons Report" released by the Department of State in June 2005 covers 150 countries, including China.

Our government estimates that every year, up to 800,000 men, women and children are trafficked across international borders into bondage. And that's across international borders.

Modern-day slavery takes many forms:
- There is domestic servitude.
- There is forced factory and farm labor.
- There is forced conscription of child soldiers.
- And there is sex slavery.

We must remember that modern-day slavery is often linked to organized crime. The FBI puts the revenue figure for organized crime in the billions. We have the drug trade, the arms trade and the people trade. Human beings are sold and resold and sold again until, because of sickness or age, they are disposed of.

China, like many other Asian countries, faces a huge problem of Chinese women and girls trafficked abroad for sexual exploitation. Chinese of both sexes migrate all over the world for low-skilled labor and a significant number of these fall victim to involuntary servitude. There are also reports of involuntary servitude (forced labor) among migrant workers moving internally within China in search of economic opportunities.

I've been talking figures and categories, but let me tell you the story of one of the lucky ones, a North Korean survivor who was trafficked in China.

In 1997, Ms. Kyeong Sook Cha fled from North Korea and in 2003 entered South Korea with two daughters and a son. But between those years, she entered a hellish netherworld—abused in domestic servitude and labor servitude, as were her two daughters.

Ms. Cha went to look for work in China when she could no longer feed her three children. Twice she was arrested by Chinese authorities, forcibly repatriated, and sent to a North Korean detention center. In China, her youngest daughter fell victim to traffickers as well. Ms. Cha traveled from village to village in China looking for her daughters, and eventually fell into debt bondage to a Korean-Chinese man who "purchased" her younger daughter to return to live with them and forced them both to labor on his farm.

After enduring the abuse of her captor, she and her daughter eventually escaped, were detained and repatriated to North Korea, escaped back into China, and began to earn money as a manager in a karaoke establishment. She searched for her older daughter by placing an advertisement in a local newspaper, and miraculously found her. Making their way through China, Vietnam and Cambodia, the reunited family took residence in South Korea two years ago.

Ms. Cha's story personifies the fates of thousands of the world's poor pushed to become migrants subjected to conditions of debt bondage, commercial sexual exploitation, and/or forced labor upon arrival in destination countries, including China.

To date, the Government of China has made limited progress in addressing key deficiencies in its efforts to address trafficking in persons. Although the government has undertaken some efforts to investigate and prosecute trafficking-related crime, much more needs to be done to detect and protect victims of trafficking.

The human rights conditions and humanitarian plight of victims trafficked to, from and through China are important concerns of Members of Congress and the whole international community. The paradigm we have created to combat trafficking in persons is a victim-centered approach that grows from a concept known as the three "Ps": prevention, protection, and prosecution.

Prevention is self-evident but underemployed. Vulnerable people, especially women and children, should be warned that promises of work abroad are often traps. The U.S. Government vigorously works to raise awareness of this issue. There is extensive information, in English and Chinese, available on the Internet regarding human trafficking, including information on ways to identify a victim and where to find resources for victims. Unfortunately, there are other Web sites that offer vital information about this global epidemic and violations of human rights that cannot be accessed by Chinese citizens. We have repeatedly urged the Chinese government to respect its international commitments to freedom of expression and to allow for the free flow of information in the media and on the Internet as a means to educate readers on human rights issues and the danger of human trafficking.

We are concerned about continued reports from NGOs and other reliable sources of an increase in the trafficking of foreign women to all parts of China as forced brides or for commercial sexual exploitation. Fueling this problem is a major gender gap—the ratio of male births to female births—that has always been present in China but has been exacerbated since the 1980s by China's draconian birth-limitation regulations. The Chinese government has recognized that this is one of the problems that fuels trafficking, but have yet to take measures to reduce the effects of the restrictive birth policy.

A bit later, you'll hear from Abraham Lee who's seen the situation first hand through his work with underground churches in Northern China. Greater efforts must be made to warn Korean women about the problem of kidnapping by some Chinese or North Korean men along the border who prey on unaccompanied women. We have called on the Chinese government to identify and protect all victims of trafficking, including North Koreans. They should not be penalized by deportation, arrest or other means because they are victims.

The government does show signs of addressing forced labor conditions among informal and formal sector laborers, which continue to be reported throughout China. For example, as Roger Plant will attest later, the Chinese government in partnership with a U.S. Government grant to ILO has embarked on a project to prevent forced labor practices in nine key provinces within the Pan-Pearl Delta region. Additionally, in the past year, the government conducted some anti-trafficking training for law enforcement officials.

In terms of protection, China has not implemented a national referral mechanism to provide trafficking victims with adequate shelter and care, nor have they adopted a national plan to address human trafficking, although they tell us one is in the works. The government's record on protection of victims of trafficking varies widely from province to province, with regional networks of support funded by the All China Women's Federation, international organizations, and local NGOs in operation across China.

To prosecute, regional cooperation is essential. The traffickers function as long as they operate beyond the law and between systems of enforcement. A good example of regional cooperation is the 2004 agreement signed by six Mekong Delta countries, including China, to hunt down and convict traffickers and sensitively repatriate victims. The Chinese Government reports that the police handled nearly 2,000 cases of trafficking in 2005, resulting in more than 3,000 women rescued. However, the lack of transparency and access to data prevents validation of these reports.

This Administration is committed to ending the trade in human beings. The Departments of State, Labor, Justice, Homeland Security, and Health and Human Services and the U.S. Agency for International Development are working together to combat this scourge both at home and abroad. Since 2001, we have contributed approximately $375 million toward anti-trafficking programs and we are seeing results.

In 2004, we saw 3000 convictions of traffickers worldwide and 39 countries amended, or passed new anti-trafficking in persons laws.

Like the struggle of the 19th century abolitionists, this 21st century struggle for freedom is one we can and must win—everywhere in the world. As President Bush said before signing the Trafficking Victims Protection Reauthorization Act of 2005,

"The trade in human beings continues in our time and we are called by conscience and compassion to bring this cruel practice to an end."

PREPARED STATEMENT OF ROGER PLANT

MARCH 6, 2006

Distinguished Members of Congress and the Administration,

I am very honoured to be with you today, and to share some information on a subject to which the ILO attaches great importance. I have been a frequent visitor to China since its government requested ILO cooperation on forced labor and human trafficking in 2002, the same year that our Special Action Program commenced its operations.

To place these activities in their proper context, I would like first to say a few words about the ILO's overall approach to the serious crime of trafficking in persons.

In May last year the ILO launched a path-breaking new report, "A Global Alliance Against Forced Labour." This provided the first global and regional estimates by an international organization of forced labor in the world today. We gave a total of 12.3 million victims of modern forced labor, of which 9.5 million are in the Asian region, and 2.45 million are victims of human trafficking. Most people are trafficked into forced labor for commercial sexual exploitation, but at least one third are also trafficked for other forms of economic exploitation. We also observed that four out of every five cases of forced labor today involve exploitation by private agents rather than the State.

These few figures set the stage for general comments about the ILO approach to human trafficking.

First, we are concerned that, while the trafficking of women and children for sexual exploitation is a particularly serious problem in the modern world, men and boys can also be trafficked for other forms of economic exploitation.

Second, when it is mainly private agents who exploit the victims of forced labor, this means that the offences of forced labor, modern slavery and slavery-like practices, are very closely linked. Indeed it is the presence of coercion (which usually takes place at the end of the trafficking cycle), which distinguishes the crime of human trafficking from that of human smuggling.

Third, we believe that the ILO's broad mandate—derived from its wide range of labor standards, and also its tripartite structure involving employers' and workers' organizations as well as governments—gives it a unique role in action against human trafficking. Whether the trafficking is for sexual or for other forms of forced labor exploitation, the ILO's main strength lies in involving labor as well as business actors, and labor institutions both inside and outside government, in broad-based action against it. This includes awareness raising, data gathering and victim identification, victim protection and law enforcement (including monitoring conditions of recruitment and employment), and return and rehabilitation of victims. Moreover, the ILO's structure makes it well placed to deal with the challenges of trafficking across the cycle between origin, transit and destination countries.

Moreover, it is important to emphasize that the ILO has two main mechanisms for dealing with problems of forced labor. It has supervisory bodies for monitoring the application of its standards, including its two Conventions on forced labor which now enjoy very widespread ratification. Second, its 1998 Declaration on Fundamental Principles and Rights at Work provides for technical assistance to member States for the promotion of core labor standards, including those on forced labor.

I now turn to the main themes I have been asked to address today: the current state of human trafficking in China; the effectiveness of ILO efforts to counter forced labor and human trafficking there; and the lessons that international and domestic anti-trafficking work may hold for policy in China.

THE CURRENT STATE OF HUMAN TRAFFICKING IN CHINA: ISSUES OF LAW AND PRACTICE

I shall not comment on the scale or extent of trafficking in and from China, as we do not have this information at hand. My comments are limited to the law and policy framework and challenges.

In recent years, there has been considerable evidence of Chinese commitment to combat trafficking, as well as smuggling. The US State Department's most recent annual Trafficking in Persons Report for 2005 refers to reports that 309 trafficking gangs were investigated, 5.043 suspected traffickers arrested, and 3,144 referred for prosecution. Anti-trafficking coordination mechanisms have been established, involving different agencies at different levels. There has been extensive distribution of information on the dangers of trafficking, as well as increased international cooperation on anti-trafficking activities. . .

As in several countries however, current penal legislation on trafficking covers only the trafficking of women and children. Article 240 of the Penal Code provides for a heavy prison sentence, plus a fine, for those persons abducting and trafficking women and children. The implication is that several of the offences covered by the definitional articles of the Palermo "Trafficking Protocol" to the United Nations Convention against Transnational Organized Crime (including forced labor or services, slavery or practices similar to slavery) are not covered by existing Chinese legislation.

A draft National Action Plan to combat trafficking is now under active discussion. It sets out some of the main challenges, if action against trafficking is henceforth to become more effective. It identifies the need for a specialist organization to coordinate anti-trafficking activities, and also a shortage of anti-trafficking institutions and personnel. More relevant research should be undertaken. International cooperation should be strengthened urgently, to deal with the increasing incidence of cross-border trafficking in women and children. And laws and regulations need to be further improved.

ILO EFFORTS TO COUNTER FORCED LABOUR AND HUMAN TRAFFICKING

ILO activities have grown steadily over the past few years. An early initiative included Yunnan province of China as part of a broader effort in the Greater Mekong Sub-region to prevent the trafficking of women and children. A specific project to prevent trafficking in girls and young women in China was then designed in close collaboration with the All China Women's Federation (ACWF) and several ministries. Commencing in 2004 with financial support from the United Kingdom, the project's main objective has been to help prevent girls and young women from ending up in unacceptable forms of work or service in China (including the "entertainment industry"), by reducing their vulnerability to trafficking. It operates in both sender and receiving provinces for potential victims of trafficking in China itself. Anhui, Henan and Hunan have been chosen as sending provinces; and Guangdong and Jiangsu as receiving provinces.

Since 2002 the ILO has been engaged in dialog and cooperation with China over forced labor concerns including trafficking in persons. In its annual report for 2003 under the ILO's Declaration on Fundamental Principles and Rights at Work the Government identified, as a difficulty with regard to the elimination of forced labor, "the lack of information and lack of capacity of responsible government institutions concerning forced labor due to trafficking". It also requested assistance with regard to broader forced labor concerns, to prepare the ground for anticipated eventual ratification of the ILO's two Conventions on forced labor. The ILO has provided assistance for proposed reforms of China's Reeducation through Labor (RETL) system, through technical seminars in China and study tours overseas. A first study tour was organized in September 2003, enabling Chinese officials to observe experience and best practices for dealing with minor offences in France, Germany, Hungary and Russia. The delegation comprised senior officials from the Ministries of Labour and Social Security, Justice and Public Security; and from the Standing Committee of People's National Congress and the Legislative Bureau of the State Council. In January 2005 a similar delegation visited Australia and Japan, to exchange experience with particular regard to community service and also measures against trafficking. An aim of these visits has been to strengthen a network of officials from key Government agencies, who can cooperate in the process of law and policy reform in the areas of forced labor and trafficking.

Since September 2004 the ILO's Special Action Programme to Combat Forced Labor has been implementing, with the Ministry of Labor and Social Security (MOLSS) as its Chinese partner agency, a project on "Forced Labor and Trafficking; the role of labor institutions in law enforcement and international cooperation in China". Supported by the US Department of Labor, the project aims to enhance the capacity of the Government of China to address the law enforcement aspects of the trafficking cycle, with activities in both China as a sender country and several European destination countries. It has components of policy advice, awareness raising and capacity building at both central and provincial levels, activities with employers' and workers' organizations, and research in the destination countries. In China, the activities have concentrated on the provinces of Fujian, Zhejiang and Jilin.

The project has already served to stimulate important debate on law and policy concerns related to trafficking, notably the difference between existing Chinese approaches and those of the Palermo Trafficking Protocol. A high-level Chinese expert reviewed all existing national legislation on forced labor, trafficking and smuggling;

as well as comparative studies on relevant concepts in national and international law. A key objective of a national seminar held under the project in April 2005 was to compare these approaches, and seek the means to harmonise Chinese law and policy with emerging international standards on trafficking.

Activities at the provincial level have had the practical objectives of training law enforcement officials, together with labor authorities, on the prevention and eradication of forced labor and trafficking. To this effect a training program held in Yanji, Jilin province in August 2005 brought together labor and public security officials from provincial and lower levels, and also representatives of recruitment agencies. This is a province of Northeastern China, bordering Russia and North Korea, with heavy unemployment of some 5 million persons. More than 100,000 migrants are currently seeking work overseas, many of them from Yanji which is an autonomous region of Chinese Korean minorities. There have been concerns that, since extensive emigration got under way in the late 1980s, Korean and Chinese recruitment agencies have colluded in deceptive recruitment mechanisms. The seminar focused on ways in which the Government can reinforce its monitoring of recruitment agencies. It also identified difficulties in effective application of existing law, in order to punish illegal recruitment agencies.

A further training workshop was held in Fujian province in November 2005, bringing together officials from Jilin, Fujian and Zheijiang provinces, along with representatives of recruitment agencies, tourism bureaus, women's organizations, labor lawyers and trade unions. Law enforcement and immigration/visa officials were also invited from France and the United Kingdom, as key destination countries for Chinese migrants from Fujian and Zheijiang. The training again focused on the prevention of trafficking, through effective monitoring of the recruitment agencies that play an important role in sending people overseas. Highlighting the deceptive methods, together with the charging of exorbitant fees, that can drive Chinese migrants into situations of severe debt bondage, participants identified the need for a major awareness raising campaign in a proposed second phase of the project.

Concurrently, SAP-FL has been carrying out a major research programme in European destination countries. Generally, there has been growing awareness that Chinese migrants can be subject to highly abusive conditions of work and transportation in the destination countries of Europe, the Middle East, the Americas and elsewhere. In the United Kingdom for example, the tragic deaths of 20 Chinese cockle pickers in early 2004 brought to light the severe forms of exploitation to which these clandestine migrants can be subjected. And in the United States, it has recently been estimated that as many as half the victims of forced labor may be ethnic Chinese.

And yet there has been very little systematic research on the subject. To fill this gap, we first issued an overview paper on the subject of Chinese migrants and forced labor in Europe. This was followed by a case study on the trafficking and exploitation of Chinese immigrants in France (currently available only in the French language, though it is now being translated into English). The study (based on 10 detailed case studies and a wide range of interviews with labour and other officials, as well as members of the Chinese community and other key informants) examines the whole cycle of recruitment and transport, as well as the living and working conditions experienced in France by clandestine Chinese migrants. It examines the complex links between the "snakehead" recruiters, either in China or overseas, and employers in the Chinese ethnic enclaves in France. High indebtedness is identified as the key factor behind the severe labor exploitation of these Chinese migrants. Some migrants are physically detained after arrival, until at least part of the debt has been paid by families back home. In other cases insolvent migrants work for an employer, who gives the wages directly to the trafficker to cover travel expenses. Fifteen-hour workdays are common, as are cases of direct physical restraint. The study estimates that it can take between 2 and 10 years for the average migrant to pay off the debt.

The French report was released with considerable publicity in Paris in June last year, and has been followed by extensive media reporting. Similar research is now under way in Italy and the United Kingdom. It has been actively solicited by our partners in the Chinese government, who see documentation of this kind as an essential ingredient of future prevention campaigns. A video film of the Chinese experience in France has recently been completed.

THE QUESTION OF EFFECTIVENESS, AND LESSONS FOR POLICY COORDINATION

How effective are our efforts? It may be early to judge, following a few years experience on a complex and sensitive subject. But during each of my visits to China, as well as several exchanges with Chinese officials abroad, I have found reason to believe that the Government, as well as our social partners in employers' and workers' organizations, are increasingly determined to grapple with the problems of human trafficking as well as smuggling, and to combat it by strengthening law enforcement and international cooperation. Only this week we are holding our first training sessions with the Chinese Employers' Confederation, in Beijing and Hanzhou respectively, on means to identify potential forced labor problems at the enterprise level and prevent their occurrence.

Despite impressive economic growth, the pressure for emigration from China remains immense. China is a labor abundant country, experiencing very high unemployment in certain regions. Some local governments actively encourage people to emigrate, regarding such emigration as a solution to local unemployment problems.

Moreover internal migrants, such as rural workers moving to the cities, can be vulnerable to trafficking for labor exploitation. There are signs that China is taking steps to respond to these challenges. Pilot reforms to the Hukou registration system, now being tested in certain cities, permit equal access to employment for migrant workers. And in 2005 China ratified the ILO's Discrimination (Employment and Occupation) Convention, No. 111 of 1958, again providing the scope for more protection for such migrants.

Internal trafficking in China, including the abduction and sale of women for forced marriage and of children for adoption, remain serious problems in China. Continued efforts are needed to clamp down on these forms of abuse, and to punish the perpetrators.

On reforms to the Reeducation through Labor system, this process is taking its time. Its reform has been incorporated in the Five-Year Legislation Plan, and a draft law regarding an alternative system of community correction has been submitted to the National Peoples' Congress. We continue to watch this matter closely.

It is important to have a realistic approach to Chinese population movements. In Europe for example, the growing presence of Chinese migrants is often viewed with concern. At a recent European meeting on illegal migration from China, the emphasis was mainly on problems of border control, fraud and visa abuse, and the use of technology such as biometrics for identifying fraudulent practices. Nevertheless—as the UK experts emphasized at our recent Fujian seminar—there can be strong demand for Chinese workers. And aspiring Chinese emigrants may pay a fortune to the snakeheads, landing themselves in severe debts, and making themselves and their families liable to violent reprisals, without even looking into the channels for lawful emigration.

For these reasons it is important in the near future to promote safe and legal migration, rather than make fruitless efforts to persuade people not to move. Awareness raising and prevention are essential measures, to complement vigorous law enforcement.

Learning from experience to date, we are now planning continued cooperation with China at both national and provincial levels. Measures to help strengthen the law and policy framework will focus on forced labor and trafficking for labour exploitation. Other aspects will focus on the training of central and provincial government officials on labor migration management, including the management of private recruitment agencies.

At the provincial level, we now plan to target more intensively the sender provinces of Fujian and Zheijiang. An awareness raising program, drawing on diverse tools including hotlines, local media and the web sites of recruitment agencies, will focus on regions already identified as at high risk for potential migrants. Other planned program components aim to improve capacities to provide education, health care and other services to victims of trafficking and labor exploitation.

A real challenge is to promote informed dialog between the governments of China and the principal destination countries for Chinese migrants, as to the means to prevent and combat forced labour and trafficking. Building on our research and data gathering, as well as the initiatives of international partners in the European Union countries and elsewhere, we see an urgent need to involve business and labour actors in this international cooperation. We aim to bring together labor institutions and authorities, law enforcement agencies and academic experts from both sides, and we hope that such an initiative will also be of interest to the United States.

Thank you for your attention.

PREPARED STATEMENT OF WENCHI YU PERKINS

MARCH 6, 2006

Senator Hagel and other distinguished members of the Commission and staff:

Thank you for choosing to focus on today's issue, "Combating Human Trafficking in China: Domestic and International Efforts."

On behalf of Vital Voices Global Partnership, I am pleased to come to you today and present on one of the world's greatest human rights violations, human trafficking, in China. Vital Voices has been at the forefront of anti-trafficking efforts since the mid 1990s. We worked with the global community to help create the "United Nations Protocol to Prevent, Suppress, and Punish Trafficking in Persons, Especially Women and Children;" and we were instrumental in the passage of the U.S. anti-trafficking legislation, "Trafficking Victims Protection Act 2000," as well as its reauthorization acts in 2003 and 2005. We have also made impacts in the region by promoting a multi-stakeholder approach to enhance government and civil society collaboration.

OVERVIEW

Human trafficking is one of the most egregious human rights violations in the 21st century. It is also a transnational crime that knows no boundaries. From North America to Asia, from Europe to Africa, no continent and no country is immune to this modern-day slavery. While the international community is still learning about the extent and gravity of this global scourge, more information is gradually coming to light. In the case of China, the situation is very serious. According to my personal experience encountering human trafficking victims in the United States, as well as the information my organization, Vital Voices Global Partnership, has collected from our partners in China, human trafficking is pervasive in China and demands increased international attention and efforts. I want to give you a couple of tangible examples of the horrific situations faced by Chinese victims of trafficking today, and then provide a general assessment of the situation within the country, especially from women and children's perspectives.

VICTIM STORIES

Ling (fictitious name), 22 years old, from Zhejiang Province, China

Ling was from Zhejiang Province. After graduating from high school, Ling began working in a factory in her neighboring city. She felt there was no hope in improving her position in life and considered herself part of the lowest class in Chinese society. After being enticed by a snakehead who told her that she could make a lot of money in the United States as a waitress, Ling was persuaded to enter the United States using false documentation. Ling first started working in a restaurant in the Midwest. She was paid approximately $500 US dollars a month and stayed in a house provided by the restaurant owner along with other girls from a similar background. Ling was making so little money that she worried about never being able to pay off her travel debt to the snakehead. Finding herself still in debt after several years of work, Ling saw an advertisement in a local Chinese newspaper and decided to take a more lucrative job at a massage parlor. Unfortunately, the massage parlor owner forced Ling to provide sexual services and when Ling refused for the first time, he threatened to send her to the authorities for deportation. Ling was suffering psychologically and physically. Her work there only came to a halt when police raided the brothel and brought Ling back to the police station. She did not speak any English, so the police enlisted the help of a local NGO involved with trafficking victim identification. Ling declined the offer by the NGO representative to stay in temporary housing until further investigation by law enforcement was completed. Ling said she was terrified that she would be deported and unable to pay off her debts, and that as a result the lives of her family in China would be threatened. As a direct result of this fear, Ling decided not to cooperate with the NGO.

Zhou (fictitious name), 17 years old, from Fujian Province, China

Zhou is one of the four children in his family with two older sisters and one younger brother. His father left home after their family farm was confiscated by the Chinese authorities because they violated the government's one-child policy. In order to find work and raise her children, Zhou's mother moved the whole family from their home village to Fuzhou City. Unfortunately, because they did not have a city residence card (hukou), Zhou and his younger brother could not receive formal schooling. This meant that at age 13, Zhou was forced to stop his formal education. By the time he turned 17, lacking a city residence card, and a sufficient education with which to find a job, Zhou had few prospects within China. As a result, Zhou's mother decided to take the risk and send him to the United States. She had witnessed many people leave the city for a life abroad and knew that there was little hope for her son to find a better life in China. She borrowed some money to pay for Zhou's travel using a snakehead (the Chinese term for human smuggler). The money was only a small portion of the total fees, and Zhou was expected to work off the remainder of his debt in the United States. Prior to arriving in the United States, Zhou learned from his mother's friends that snakeheads often threaten families back in China if debts are not paid on time. Snakeheads almost always operate as part of a large-scale crime syndicate, and their tactics are infamously brutal. This pressure was instilled within Zhou even before he left China. Upon arrival in the United States, Zhou was detained by a customs official for using false documents and was put into a detention center. With the assistance of a legal aid pro bono attorney, Zhou was released from U.S. immigration custody while his case was in the proceedings. Once released, he found himself terrified by the prospect of not being able to pay off his substantial debts and the penalties back home that might ensue. These fears were compounded when he received news that the snakehead had already begun calling his mother in China. Knowing the potential consequences which would likely arise from being deported, penniless, back to China, Zhou chose not to report back to the court as required. He decided that living illegally and in squalid conditions was preferable to endangering the life of his mother. As illustrated, this fear tactic employed by traffickers is extremely effective at keeping victims in exploitive situations, and fearful of the authorities.

HUMAN TRAFFICKING FROM, WITHIN, AND INTO CHINA

Human trafficking from China

The two stories I shared above were from victims I encountered while working for an immigration legal aid organization in the Midwest. Their stories are similar to those of many other victims of trafficking who originate from China. The majority of Chinese victims start as voluntary migrants, who have been convinced by their neighbors and relatives that life would be much better in other countries. Contrary to finding a land of wealth and opportunity, however, most of them are grossly exploited throughout the migration process. Without proper immigration documents, they end up making little to no money, working in horrific conditions in sweatshop factories or as forced prostitutes, and remain under constant threat from their traffickers. Even after their arrival in the United States, their distrust of law enforcement, based on past experience with corrupt government officials in China, forces them to remain vulnerable and exploited by their traffickers.

The physical and psychological control of these vulnerable trafficking victims by the organized syndicates is intense enough to force them to engage in illicit activities. Most victims have a deep-seated fear for the safety of their family back home. This is illustrated by a 16-year-old girl who I encountered after she had been detained at immigration facilities. The girl was meticulously saving every single dollar that she was given by the authorities and sending the money back to China, because "every dollar could help my mother pay off the debt." Even with such devoted saving, it is often impossible to completely pay off these debts, as snakeheads impose ridiculously high interest rates. Compounding the problem is the fact that many of the exploited are minors under the age of 18, who are easily manipulated.

Most victims come from coastal provinces such as Fujian, Zhejiang, Jiangsu, and Guangdong; however, the continued trafficking of ethnic minorities from China's southwest, primarily Yunnan and Guangxi Provinces, to the Mekong Sub-region is also of concern. Many international organizations have been working in the Mekong Sub-region for a long time to help repatriate victims and raise awareness, yet continued efforts are still needed.

Chinese victims of trafficking are forced into sexual and labor exploitation. Not only are they psychologically and physically abused by their traffickers, they are held in indentured servitude or as bonded labor. Some of them leave their homes, believing that they will marry men in Taiwan, Japan, Hong Kong, Malaysia, or other Asian countries, but instead fall victim to trafficking, becoming forced prostitutes or laborers. Some of them become mail-order brides, only to find out too late that their husbands are different from what the marriage brokers claimed, and often fall prey to abuse. In such cases, their uncertain immigration status and fear of losing child custody often leads many women to endure extremely abusive and dehumanizing situations simply because they feel they have no other options.

Most Chinese victims of trafficking, because of their illegal immigration status or because they are involved in illegal activities, are automatically categorized as criminals by law enforcement. Without acknowledgment of the exploitive situation they are in, most victims are put directly into detention centers without proper screening or identification. Once they are placed in detention facilities, it can take up to years for them to be deported back to China because local Chinese embassies and consulates often ignore requests for deportation travel documents by destination country immigration officials. The problems for victims being deported back to China are magnified if they have been trafficked to Taiwan. Political tension between the two sides, as well as the lack of an official repatriation process, only exacerbates an already difficult process. Victims trafficked from China to Taiwan are primarily women who were trafficked for sexual exploitation. These women find themselves detained in Taiwan's immigration detention facilities for prolonged periods of time, to the degree that some are forced to give birth to children while being held in confinement.

Many of the victims want to go back to China simply because they do not want to stay in the detention facilities indefinitely. However, many more fear deportation because it is a crime in China to leave the country without the government's permission. Some say that they will need to serve time in jail upon returning home and that the length of jail time will depend on how much money they can raise for a bribe. I have heard stories that those deported back to China without money for a bribe are stripped of clothes and beaten in jail.

Human trafficking within China

Human trafficking within China is also pervasive. In addition to the abduction of women and children for sexual exploitation, it is said that trafficking for forced marriage has been increasing since the 1980's. Most of the women are abducted and taken to rural areas for purchase by older men or by those who are of a low position in society and have difficulty finding a willing partner. In fact, the practice of forced marriage is not a new development in China. Throughout history, many women from "better" families were abducted to marry heads of gangs or tribal leaders in remote areas. This has led to greater societal acceptance of this practice. Recently, it is believed that trafficking for forced marriage has increased due to the imbalance in the numbers of women to men as a result of the one-child policy and Chinese society's traditional preference for sons. According to the report, An Absence of Choice, men currently outnumber women with a ratio of 13:10, and in some rural populations the disparity is even greater. According to a Vital Voices' partner in China, some Chinese even think forced marriage is a way to prevent rape and sexual assault in the community, since it assures that the sexual needs of these men are being met. Therefore, the practice of forced marriage is tolerated in some less developed areas and has been flourishing in recent years.

Another trafficking situation that has arisen in part from the one-child policy is the trafficking of infants, most under the age of one. Baby boys are often trafficked to families unable to have a son, and baby girls are sold, often by professional rings, to orphanages who profit from overseas adoptions. This practice is bolstered by Chinese culture's traditional preference for boys. Baby trafficking has drawn wide attention in China, and the government is starting to crack down on such cases.

Another human trafficking practice within China that has not received enough attention is trafficking for labor exploitation. Migrant worker issues in China have drawn world attention, as the abundance of cheap Chinese labor has made the country the world's largest sweatshop. Most of the factories in the wealthy south employ migrant workers from the poorer west or north. Similarly, most of the migrant worker voluntarily move to the south for factory jobs but become exploited laborers. According to Verité, a non-profit organization monitoring China's labor conditions, 70 percent of the migrant workers in the Pearl River Delta are females under the age of 25 and are extremely vulnerable to all forms of exploitation. Most of them migrate to the south being told that they will be paid according to the contract they sign and that they will be protected by national labor laws. China's labor laws stipulate that all workers shall work no more than 8 hours a day, 44 hours a week. In reality, forced overtime is almost a norm in these factories. According to the China Daily, last November a Sichuan woman working in Guangzhou fell into a coma and passed away after being forced to work for 24 hours non-stop in order to finish orders. Furthermore, while the average monthly pay for a woman migrant worker is about Renminbi 300–500 (US $37.5—$62.5) in Guangdong province, some of the factories do not even pay minimum wage and others illegally deduct meal and dormitory fees from workers' pay. China's migrant labor exploitation in the south has been discussed widely, and I am grateful that the Commission has held several hearings and roundtables on this topic before. However, this issue has not been explored in the context of human trafficking, and most people do not realize that these workers come to the south because they are told that they can make more money to better support their families in rural areas. I urge the Commission and the U.S.

State Department's Office to Combat and Monitor Trafficking in Persons to pay special attention to this form of human trafficking.

Human trafficking into China

Human trafficking for forced marriage also occurs across borders when Chinese men seek brides from neighboring and often poorer countries. The most frequent offences happen with women trafficked from Burma, Cambodia, and particularly Vietnam. News stories about Vietnamese girls trafficked into China for forced marriage or sexual exploitation appear regularly in both local and international press. In response to this growing problem, the Chinese and Vietnamese governments have participated in several joint-projects and agreements over the past few years in an effort to stop this form of trafficking in women and children.

The Chinese government has taken steps to confront the trafficking problems in its southwest region. However it continues to turn a blind eye on the equally problematic situation that has emerged in the northeast. Due to the constant threat of starvation, which began with the famines of the mid 1990's, North Koreans have been fleeing into China. Rather than designating them as refugees, the Chinese government continues to view these people as economic and illegal migrants, and to deport them back to the Democratic Peoples Republic of Korea (DPRK). This leaves this vulnerable population, the majority of which are women, especially susceptible to both sexual and labor exploitation. Almost all illegal North Koreans in China would rather endure abusive working conditions as domestic servants, nannies or even wives than return to the DPRK, where leaving the country without the government's permission could lead to a death sentence.

While the previous two areas suffer primarily from the trafficking of women, there have also been news reports about men being trafficked from Kyrgyzstan into China for forced labor, especially to the predominantly Muslim Xinjiang region. There has also been documentation of Xinjiang children, who are from the native Uighur minority, being trafficked throughout China as forced beggars and thieves.

ANTI-TRAFFICKING EFFORTS IN CHINA

The Chinese government's anti-trafficking work falls under the jurisdiction of the Ministry of Public Security. In 2005, the Bureau of Public Security of Dongxing Prefecture, Guangxi Province established a shelter, the Transitional Center for Rescued Foreign Women and Children. The center provides care for rescued Vietnamese women and children. China already has in place extensive laws to prosecute trafficking crimes. Despite these prosecutorial elements being in place, the government has made an insufficient effort at protection and rehabilitation of victims, particularly those who are deported back to China and foreign nationals who have been trafficked into the country. While the Transitional Center for Rescued Foreign Women and Children is a step in the right direction, much more needs to be done in the effort to formally address the issue of victim protection and rehabilitation. China's prevention work is limited to certain provinces rather than being comprehensive. This means that some affected regions are not receiving crucial preventative education, and that the cycle of trafficking can continue unchecked.

While the greatest responsibility of anti-trafficking activities is currently shouldered by the government, there are several local groups that are working on this issue. The All-China Women's Federation (ACWF) currently provides legal assistance to victims of trafficking in China. Vital Voices also works with independent local Chinese NGOs that provide legal assistance to victims of trafficking for forced marriage or domestic servitude.

In addition to local NGOs and state groups, there are several international organizations working on join anti-trafficking projects with the Chinese government and the All-China Women's Federation. They include the UNESCO, the UNICEF, and the ILO.

RECOMMENDATIONS

The Congress can play a vital role to help address the modern-day slavery from, within and to China. On behalf of Vital Voices Global Partnership, I have the following recommendations:

1. Encourage specialized training for law enforcement and judges

Successful prosecutions and investigations are the only means to halt human traffickers. The Chinese government has done quite a lot through the Ministry of Public Security and the anti-trafficking coordinating office. More law enforcement training should be available at the provincial and county levels so anti-trafficking efforts are not limited to the central government.

2. Avail greater resources to promote collaboration between government and NGOs in China

In line with training for law enforcement and judges, capacity building for NGOs needs to occur at all levels. This will allow them to complement government efforts while providing professional services and making positive changes. Additional leadership training for the emerging NGO leaders in China is a crucial component of the training that needs to occur. Toward these efforts, groups should conduct nationwide training for their employees and work with other organizations, both international and local, to facilitate collaborative efforts between the government and NGOs in victim identification and assistance.

3. Call on international business community to help change and prevent the practices of exploiting trafficked migrant labor

In addition to government and NGOs, the business sector is vital in successful anti-trafficking efforts. Many garment, toy, and other labor-intensive manufacturing factories are contractors or sub-contractors of international brands. Most international companies can work with their contractors in China to ensure that migrant workers are not exploited and that employers abide by China's labor laws.

4. Authorize funding to support large-scale awareness raising campaigns to prevent human trafficking

Most Chinese citizens at risk of being trafficked do not realize the potential danger involved in the migration process. Many of them feel hopeless in their community and fantasize about life overseas or in the large cities. It is vitally important that the government partners with popular public figures to launch large-scale campaigns targeting at-risk youths and informing them about the reality of life overseas. This should also include information on available assistance, such as support networks and hotlines. In areas highly vulnerable to human trafficking, such as Yunnan, Guangxi, Fujian, Zhejiang, Henan, Gansu, Shanxi, Jilin, the autonomous regions and those with significant populations of ethnic minorities, government and NGOs should carry out targeted and focused campaigns.

5. Urge the Chinese government to reconsider government policies resulting in irregular migration and exploitation of migrants

China's one-child policy, household registration policy, and the control of citizen exit and entry policy have resulted in irregular migration and a large underground market for organized syndicates to maneuver and exploit vulnerable migrants. While we understand that the government is gradually changing some of these policies, and we welcome those changes, the severe social consequences that resulted from earlier policies need to be carefully dealt with.

6. Analyze the various forms of trafficking and the best practices of reintegrating trafficked women into their community and providing them with practical living skills

There have been some legal research and field studies on trafficking in China. However, the studies are limited to certain regions and certain types of trafficking. The trafficking for forced marriage is under-addressed; the trafficking for forced labor within and from China is also a greater challenge that deserves more than labor rights advocates' attention, especially when most exploited migrant workers are women. Migrant labor trafficking should be discussed in the human trafficking context as well.

Studies should be conducted and best practices identified from the various projects currently being carried out on smaller scales. Examples of some best practices include the recent pilot project conducted by All China Women's Federation and UNICEF, which set up women's activity centers in Sichuan Province for the reintegration of trafficked women. These centers seek to equip victims with practical living skills and have proven to be very successful. This type of pilot project needs to be identified, supported and then replicated by the government and the international community.

Vital Voices plays a key role in designing and implementing the multi-stakeholder approach to the trafficking challenge worldwide. In East Asia, we have successfully changed policies and laws in Japan by engaging multiple stakeholders. Soon we will be implementing another program in Bangkok adopting the same approach. China's tactics for combating human trafficking are still sporadic and disjointed. The Chinese central government is beginning to take seriously the threat of human trafficking. Nonetheless, efforts must occur on all levels and utilize all sectors of society, including business and civil society. Similar to Japan and Thailand, we believe that China will also need a comprehensive and multi-stakeholder approach to tackle the complex issue of human trafficking. Only by combating trafficking on multiple levels and involving as many stakeholders as possible will China be able to effectively address this horrendous problem.

Thank you.

PREPARED STATEMENT OF ABRAHAM LEE

MARCH 6, 2006

I. INTRODUCTION

Crossing Borders is a faith-based organization committed to maintaining a sustainable and viable presence in Northeast China to aid the plight of North Koreans fleeing the oppression and suffering of the North Korea regime. Our vision is to see the refugees under our care reestablish their sense of self-worth, self-respect and their sense of hope by providing food, clothes, shelter, and medicine with love and care.

II. STATE OF NORTH KOREA

Information from within the Democratic People's Republic of Korea (DPRK) confirms ongoing suspicions of continuing famine-like conditions particularly in rural areas along the Tumen River border with Northeast China. Reports indicate that proposed rations purported to be distributed to workers and citizens beginning in October 2005 have not been made available and the North Korean people continue to go hungry. The lack of food and accompanying malnutrition appear to be substantial factors in the spread of tuberculosis among villagers. In addition, as the testimony of the growing number of defectors out of North Korea have confirmed, the government of the DPRK continues unabated as a regime committed to the suppression of human rights and freedom within its borders. Its citizens live under constant fear and threat of brutality including possible detention in notorious political prison camps and even summary execution. Repatriated refugees who were unsuccessful in their attempts to escape to China and evangelical Christians are particularly susceptible to intense persecution.

The extreme famine of the late 1990's triggered a mass exodus of refugees into China in search of food and an opportunity for survival. With little improvement in the basic living standard of most North Koreans, the flow of refugees continues to remain steady. Especially in towns along the Chinese border, increased access to information from returning refugees and visitors from China entice citizens to pursue a better life across the border. In addition, while many still attempt the treacherous journey through the mountains or across icy rivers to reach China, the border has become more porous and accessible often only requiring a bribe to a border guard of approximately 200RMB ($25) per crossing. Reports indicate that meals inside North Korea consist of fried corn gruel and boiled weeds while going hungry is often the norm. Rice is virtually unavailable.

III. REFUGEE VULNERABILITY

The combination of extreme hunger, potential economic opportunity and easier access motivates refugees to abandon family and risk their lives to enter China. It also provides human traffickers the perfect opportunity to exploit this desperate situation. Although the numbers are difficult to quantify, reports indicate that as many as 70–80 percent of all North Korean women who enter China illegally are victims of trafficking. Refugees in the care of Crossing Borders often admit to having been lied to or abused during their journey to or during their subsequent stay in China. In response to the question "Have you been lied to?" or "Have you been abused?" a common answer is "many times" or "more times than I can count."

North Korean women are particularly susceptible to physical and sexual abuse. Chinese farmers are often unable to find spouses because of their low social status as well as the migration of an already sparse population of potential women to the cities. The narrow probability of finding a wife leads many Chinese men to seek a companion among the vulnerable female population of North Korea. For the cost of $50 a trafficker will pose as a businessman and enter North Korea on behalf of a Chinese farmer. The trafficker will entice reluctant women by offering food, clothes, shelter and a "better life" in exchange for an arranged marriage with a Chinese suitor. Seeing no other options and often with the slim hope of providing for the family left behind in North Korea many women agree to the arrangement.

The United Nations Protocol to Prevent, Suppress and Punish Trafficking in Persons defines trafficking in persons as: "the recruitment, transportation, transfer, harboring or receipt of persons, by means of . . . the abuse of power or of a position of vulnerability or of the giving or receiving of payments or benefits to achieve the consent of a person having control over another person, for the purpose of exploitation."[1]

North Koreans are in the ultimate position of vulnerability with the only alternative to following a trafficker into China being starvation, suffering and possibly death. Knowing this, traffickers take advantage of the dire situations of young North Korean women and coerce them into agreeing to the arranged marriage. Many of the promises of a "better life" are never fulfilled and many of the arranged marriages are to physically disabled or alcoholic husbands with the end result often being abandonment or physical abuse.

Traffickers also prey on refugees by offering jobs in China and lying about what they can offer them. Ms. Kim's[2] family was approached immediately by traffickers and her mother was given promises that they could provide a good job in a factory for her daughter. In addition, Ms. Kim would be able to regularly send money home to help the family. In fear of following these men into a foreign country and having to leave her family behind, Ms. Kim protested and refused to go. However, her mother encouraged her saying, "Trust these people. It will be best for our family." When she finally arrived in China there was no factory, no job and no money. She was immediately sold and sexually abused by the man who bought her.

So-Young was only 15 years old when she and a friend crossed the river from North Korea into China. They were approached immediately by Chinese men. They promised the girls wages of 300RMB ($36) per month if they worked for them. It was enough for the young girls to agree. The two thought surely they were too young to be sold as a wife or slave. The next morning however, So-Young awoke to discover that her friend had been sold. That was the last time she ever saw her. So-Young was forced to work and wait to grow taller in order to be sold. After four months, the first buyer came to claim his bride—a 40 year old Chinese man. "I was so disgusted at that point, all I could do was cry out, 'Heavenly Lord,'" she said. "I never heard the phrase before, I never heard of Jesus. But I had a slight conception of a heavenly place so I cried out." She managed to evade attempts to sell her by stubbornly refusing to go. After repeated failed attempts to sell her, So-Young was transported again to a new home and later came to realize she was simply being moved to meet a new buyer. She soon discovered that the mistress of the house was intending to sell her to help pay for college. So-Young recalled, "She said she would no longer be able to take care of me, and that I should marry a Chinese man." Immediately, So-Young alerted one of the deacons of a local underground church in the village who had compassion for her situation and secretly ministered to her. Together they planned her escape. The next morning she ran away. After three years as a refugee however, So-Young was discovered and sent back to North Korea where she faced insufferable imprisonment for six months before escaping to China a second time. She was caught by traffickers again, and this time was raped by her sellers. Eventually, she was sold to a Chinese man who also raped her multiple times before she was able to run away. Today So-Young remains in hiding and faces daily the possibility of being captured again. "There are many people coming out of North Korea," she said. "But they don't have anywhere to go and no other choice but to go that route [into China]."

Unfortunately, the desperation of many North Korean women makes them susceptible to being trafficked more than once. HyunJoo first escaped to China in March 2004. She was sold and forced into an abusive relationship with a Chinese man. Unhappy and looking for a means of escape, she was able to make contact with a local pastor and entered into one of our Restore Life[3] shelters. Against our advice, she attempted to flee to South Korea and was repatriated back to North Korea. She attempted to return to China in early 2005 but chronic pain in her lower extremities forced her to abort the attempt. Through our NKM ministry[4] we were able to send funds for her to obtain medical attention. She entered China in December 2005 and subsequently was captured and trafficked to a Chinese buyer approximately 4 hours outside of Shenyang.[5] We were unaware of her exact whereabouts until we received a phone call on February 16, 2006. She called requesting assistance and hoping to reenter a RL shelter. We are currently working feverishly to help her escape. She

---

[1] http://www.unodc.org/unodc/en/trafficking_protocol.html.
[2] All names of refugees have been changed to conceal their identity and protect their safety.
[3] Restore Life (RL) ministry is the main refugee support mission of Crossing Borders.
[4] Crossing Borders sends in approximately five teams of Korean-Chinese citizens per month into North Korea to provide assistance as part of its NKM ministry.
[5] Capital of Liaoning Province in Northeast China.

is just one of many who attempt this journey even if it means having to suffer again through the agony of being a trafficking victim.

Children are also the unintended victims of many of these trafficking stories. The children in our 2nd Wave shelters[6] have a Chinese father and North Korean mother. Their mothers were subsequently repatriated, re-trafficked or have simply disappeared with the father unable or unwilling to take care of the children. Mina is an 8 year old young girl who studies hard in school and who loves to smile and laugh. Four years ago her North Korean mother disappeared apparently having abandoned her young daughter and her dying Chinese father. With his deteriorating health, her father was unable to care for her and Mina suffered in poverty and inattention. Thankfully, she was able to enter our shelter and with Chinese citizenship has a hope for a brighter future through constant love, care, and an opportunity to attend school. Unfortunately, many of these young children never get this opportunity and are often left to fend for themselves. The difference between finding hope in a local church and becoming a victim of trafficking is great but the probability of finding safety is slim. The road into China is littered with potential dangers including human traffickers, Chinese authorities and even North Korean security agents. But while still relatively few, the number of refugees able to find protection in the care of evangelical Christians and other organizations is growing.

IV. CHINESE GOVERNMENT PERSECUTION

In 2002, along the streets of Yanji City[7] just 30 kilometers from the North Korean border, it was not uncommon for visitors to encounter North Korean refugees begging for food and money in the streets. Many of these refugees were children. However, by 2005, there were absolutely no refugees visible in and around the city streets of Yanji City.

Beginning in 2003, it appears that the Chinese government increased its efforts to hunt down and repatriate North Korean refugees as well as persecute and arrest those who attempted to provide assistance to refugees. This increase in pressure has forced refugees to go deeper into hiding and become even more dependent on the network of organizations devoted to giving them help. According to local reports, as many as 40 refugees per month were being repatriated by Chinese authorities through the Tumen Detention Center in 2003.

Through our NKM ministry we were able to gain intimate details of what happens to repatriated refugees after being caught by Chinese police. Mrs. Huh's son and younger sister fled to China and found refuge in a local church. However, a raid by Chinese police resulted in their detention and forced repatriation back to North Korea. Mrs. Huh's son and younger sister were summarily executed by firing squad for allegedly committing criminal acts while in China. Unofficially, the real reason for their execution was their contact with the local church in China and for their conversion to Christianity. These types of stories of complicity by the Chinese government and the severe punishment of repatriated North Koreans have been well documented.

As has been widely reported, China has failed to live up to its obligations under the 1951 Convention relating to the Status of Refugees and its 1967 Protocol. China continues to stand by its position that North Koreans are economic migrants and thus their expulsion is a valid exercise of their right to enforce illegal immigration policy. With the definitive accounts of conditions within North Korea, it is obvious that North Koreans are fleeing famine and persecution and not as economic migrants. China is in clear violation of its obligations by failing to render aid, by forcibly repatriating refugees and by blocking access to refugees by the United Nations High Commissioner for Refugees (UNHCR).[8] In addition, the entire governmental system of enforcement continues to be saturated in corruption and inconsistency. The staff at Crossing Borders observed there appears to be an increase in governmental activity and persecution in the winter months leading up to the New Year. Further inquiry leads us to believe that the increase at least in part and probably in whole is due to the coming festive season of New Year's and the seeking of bribes by local officials to supplement their income in preparation for the coming celebration. In winter 2003, the Chinese government cracked down on local churches for harboring North Korean refugees. Fines were assessed and local pastors were

---

[6] One of the ministries of Crossing Borders committed to giving hope and opportunity to needy children.

[7] Capital of the Yanbian Autonomous Prefecture in Northeast China.

[8] Under its agreement obligations, China is required to grant the UNHCR unimpeded access to refugees in China.

banned from entering church grounds. Recently, around Christmas 2005, Yanji Church received a fine of 60,000RMB ($7500).[9]

Most regrettably, one of our local shelters was forced to shut down because of Chinese governmental pressure. We maintained a shelter of three North Korean teenagers until October 23rd of last year when we received word that one of the teenager's parents were attempting to flee to South Korea and wanted to take their son with them. After his departure from the shelter we continued to maintain it until December 16th when the remaining teens and their caretaker were forced to abandon the shelter after three Chinese policemen had knocked on the door earlier in the day. Only one of the teens was present at home at the time and wisely did not answer the door. The local staff person responsible for the administration of this shelter was forced to go into hiding into the countryside for approximately one month leaving behind his wife. The breach in security forced us to close down the shelter. Later we learned that the family attempting to escape to South Korea was captured by Chinese officials. Under interrogation, they proffered the name of the local staff person and the location of the shelter. The whereabouts of the family are still unknown. If captured, the local staff person who is a Chinese citizen would most likely have been imprisoned, interrogated and/or fined a substantial amount.

The network of local Chinese citizens is an invaluable part of the ongoing work to help rescue and restore North Korean refugees. Without their assistance, the work of Crossing Borders and other organizations would be impossible. Our status as foreign aid workers offers some form of limited protection against the Chinese authorities, but these local workers have no such protections and risk their very lives and freedom in helping North Koreans.

V. CONCLUSION

Crossing Borders is committed to providing assistance to the continuing flow of North Korean refugees that enter China everyday. Although there are potentially one thousand refugees in need of assistance within our network of local churches, we are only able to directly help a small fraction of them. The Chinese government and its actions against North Koreans stand as an enormous roadblock to achieving our mission. Understandably, the situation is a complicated one, but the United States has an obligation to take a stand against China and North Korea as perpetuators of evil and suffering against a weak and vulnerable population. The Chinese government has done little to combat the network of traffickers that exist along the North Korean border and fails to comply with its obligations to protect North Koreans within its country. We hope that provision may be made to provide asylum for these suffering people and that the United States would be the leader in providing hope to a people starving for a better life.

PREPARED STATEMENT OF HON. CHUCK HAGEL, A U.S. SENATOR FROM NEBRASKA, CHAIRMAN, CONGRESSIONAL-EXECUTIVE COMMISSION ON CHINA

MARCH 6, 2006

The Congressional-Executive Commission on China meets today to examine human trafficking in China. The Commission will also consider domestic and international efforts to help stop human trafficking in and through China and to help rehabilitate victims of trafficking.

Human trafficking in China is a serious problem. According to a 2002 United Nations Children's Fund (UNICEF) estimate, there are approximately 250,000 victims of trafficking in China. Traffickers are increasingly linked to organized crime and specialize in abducting girls and women both for the bridal market in China's poorest areas and for sale as prostitutes in urban areas. North Korean refugees are an especially vulnerable group. Today's Administration witness, Ambassador John Miller, has estimated that 80 to 90 percent of the refugees from North Korea, particularly women and children, end up as trafficking victims.

The Chinese government has publicly acknowledged the seriousness of the problem and has taken steps to stop trafficking and aid victims. Chinese experts and officials have cooperated with international agencies including the International Labor Organization (ILO) and UNICEF to combat trafficking. China's Law on the Protection of Rights and Interests of Women outlaws trafficking, and Article 240 of the Criminal Law outlines harsh penalties for those convicted of human trafficking related crimes.

---

[9] Although this fine was unrelated to involvement with North Koreans it is here to illustrate the increase in bribes during the winter months.

These steps reflect a serious effort, but the Chinese government needs to do more. The Commission is concerned that China fell from "Tier 2" to "Tier 2 Watch Status" in the State Department's Trafficking in Persons Report for 2005 because of inadequate protection of trafficking victims. The Chinese government must uphold international agreements and grant the U.N. High Commission for Refugees unimpeded access to screen the refugee petitions of North Koreans in China. The Chinese government has not signed the U.N. Protocol to Prevent, Suppress, and Punish Trafficking in Persons, Especially Women and Children.

The United States can do more. In its 2005 Annual Report, the Commission recommended that the President and Congress continue to support international programs to build law enforcement capacity to prevent trafficking in and through China, and additionally should develop and fund programs led by U.S.-based Non-Governmental Organizations (NGO) that focus on the protection and rehabilitation of victims, especially legal and educational assistance programs. But the Chinese government must become more open to cooperation with foreign NGOs.

To help us better understand the human trafficking problem in China, and international and domestic efforts to fight trafficking and assist victims, we turn to our witnesses.

Representative Chris Smith has been a leader in Congressional efforts to combat trafficking worldwide and assist victims of trafficking. Earlier this year, President Bush signed into law Representative Smith's third anti-trafficking bill, the Trafficking Victims Protection Reauthorization Act of 2005. This new law provides significant additional anti-trafficking and protection measures for victims and potential victims of trafficking.

Representative Smith is Vice Chairman of the House International Relations Committee, and Chairman of the International Relations subcommittee on Africa, Global Human Rights, and International Operations. The Commission is very pleased that Mr. Smith will be making a statement at today's hearing.

Speaking on behalf of the Administration will be Ambassador John R. Miller, who is Director of the State Department's Office to Monitor and Combat Trafficking in Persons and Senior Advisor to Secretary of State Condoleezza Rice on human trafficking. From 1985 to 1993, Mr. Miller served in the U.S. House of Representatives from the state of Washington. While in Congress, Mr. Miller held a seat on the Committee on International Relations and was a member of the Congressional Human Rights Caucus.

After Ambassador Miller, we will hear from a distinguished panel of experts who will share their knowledge and expertise. Mr. Roger Plant will lead Panel Two. Mr. Plant is the Head of the ILO's Special Action Program to Combat Forced Labor. Mr. Plant has been a leading investigator and activist on forced labor and modern slavery for more than 30 years. Prior to joining the ILO Mr. Plant worked with the Asian Development Bank, United Kingdom Department for International Development; Inter-American Development Bank, United Nations Officer of the High Commissioner for Human Rights; Shell International, Danish International Development Agency, and several international human rights NGOs.

Ms. Wenchi Yu Perkins will provide perspectives on the problem of human trafficking to and from China. Ms. Perkins is the Director of Anti-Trafficking and Human Rights Programs at Vital Voices. Prior to joining Vital Voices, Ms. Perkins worked with victims of trafficking and conducted training for law enforcement and NGOs in the Midwest. She was also a foreign policy assistant in Taiwan's parliament and worked in the Taiwan representative office in Chicago. She has an MA in International Relations from the University of Chicago and a BA in Political Science from National Taiwan University.

Finally, Mr. Abraham Lee will testify to the Commission on the problems faced by North Korean refugees in China. Mr. Lee is Director of Public Affairs for Crossing Borders, an NGO devoted to assisting North Korean refugees in Northeast China. Mr. Lee has been in China for the past three years working with North Korean refugees and teaching college English. He received his BA in Economics from the University of Maryland in 1999 and his JD from the University of Maryland School of Law in 2002.

We welcome all of our witnesses today and appreciate their time and presentations.

PREPARED STATEMENT OF HON. JAMES A. LEACH, A REPRESENTATIVE FROM IOWA, CO-CHAIRMAN, CONGRESSIONAL-EXECUTIVE COMMISSION ON CHINA

MARCH 6, 2006

Chairman Hagel, fellow members of the Commission,

I am pleased to join the Commission this afternoon in convening this important hearing on trafficking in persons in the People's Republic of China. Under the provisions of Public Law No. 106–286, the Act which created this Commission, the CECC continues today its monitoring of Chinese government policy and practice on this important cross-border issue. I join you in welcoming our distinguished panels of witnesses, including my colleague Representative Chris Smith of New Jersey, who is an acknowledged expert on the issue that is the subject of our inquiry today, and former Representative John Miller, with whom I served for a number of years in the House.

Ambassador Miller's work on the urgent matter of international trafficking in human beings since his appointment to the State Department in 2004 deserves our respect, because this crime against human dignity is unconscionable anywhere it occurs. The comprehensive and excellent annual Human Trafficking Repot that Ambassador Miller's office produces each year is a sobering assessment of transnational criminality and the profound human suffering that it causes.

The Chinese government has undertaken a number of positive steps to try to curb trafficking in human beings in and through China. As the Commission's Annual Report for 2005 notes, these steps include supporting some international initiatives and enacting domestic laws to establish a framework for the investigation and prosecution of traffickers. But trafficking in persons—particularly of women and female children—remains great in China, and the toll on its victims greater. In addition to the Chinese government's own domestic efforts, international cooperation to arrest and prosecute traffickers and assist the victims is crucial.

I look forward to hearing the expert testimony of Congressman Smith, Ambassador Miller, and our witnesses representing international and non-governmental organizations.

Thank you.

PREPARED STATEMENT OF HON. SAM BROWNBACK, A U.S. SENATOR FROM KANSAS, MEMBER, CONGRESSIONAL-EXECUTIVE COMMISSION ON CHINA

MARCH 6, 2006

Mr. Chairman, I commend you for calling this hearing and am pleased that the Congressional-Executive Commission on China (CECC) is taking a hard look at human trafficking in China.

China is certainly not the only country dealing with the scourge of human trafficking, in fact, the State Department's 2005 Trafficking in Persons (TIP) Report details the trafficking situation in 150 countries. But what makes the tragedy of human trafficking in China all the more unjustifiable is that a good portion of the human trafficking in China is internal only to China, and is fueled by its own social policies.

I am talking about China's one-child policy.

This is an Orwellian policy that over the past 25 years has created a lost generation of daughters and wives-some say as many as 40–60 million by the end of this decade. The International Labor Organization states that the trends in trafficking in China are distinctive because most of it occurs for marriage or adoption. This gender imbalance means that women have become a commodity in China-a commodity that can be bought and sold. The TIP report notes that "significant numbers of Chinese women are trafficked internally for forced marriage." We don't know the exact number of women who are sentenced to a life of degradation and servitude-but even one is one too many.

Boys are vulnerable as well under this system. UNICEF estimates the going price for a baby boy in China is about US $3,000. Again, this is based on a Chinese Government policy that dictates the number of children a couple can have. The result is families that are deprived of daughters, infant girls that are killed before they are born (girls account for 70 percent of abortions in China), and baby girls that are routinely abandoned. And if a girl is lucky enough to survive a few years, she is then vulnerable as a commodity on the marriage or labor market.

The TIP report states that despite some increased law enforcement activity, China's enforcement of laws and prosecution of traffickers is "inadequate." I would also add to that assessment that one of the real problems that feeds trafficking in China is rampant corruption within the Chinese Government-including law enforcement-and the lack of a rule of law in which an independent judiciary would hear trafficking and forced labor cases. I suspect that if China had such a system, many of the cases those courts would hear today would involve Chinese officials abusing their position of power to traffic women and children.

Sadly, those are not the cases that we see in China today.

I am also deeply concerned about the plight of North Korean women in China. The ongoing food and economic crisis in North Korea has driven an estimated 200,000 North Koreans to northeast China, fleeing for their lives from prison camps or political persecution. Once in China, North Koreans seek work and shelter with relatives, acquaintances or strangers, moving from time to time to avoid being detected by the Chinese authorities. Traffickers seek out North Korean women to exploit at river crossings, train stations or markets. Women who cross the border alone are often picked up as soon as they reach the other side by traffickers who lie in wait for them. Many arrive hungry and desperate and become easy targets for the traffickers.

Because of discriminatory social status, women without trusted family members in China have little choice but to rely on strangers for assistance and information. In such situations, North Korean women and children, who are cheaper in price than Chinese women and who have no legal protection in China, easily fall prey to sexual exploitation. These women are abducted and sold, either to men as informal wives or concubines or to the sex industry. Because of the growing gender disparity, many men have difficulty finding a wife, particularly in rural areas. In this context, North Korean women are mostly sold to Chinese farmers who are considered undesirable to Chinese women because of their poverty, age, or disability.

The repressive government of North Korea does not comply with the minimum standards for the elimination of trafficking and is not making efforts to do so. China does not even meet minimal standards under the Refugee Convention to reduce the kidnapping, deportation and sexual exploitation of North Korean women living under these inhumane circumstances. The UN High Commission on Human Rights ought to take an active approach for North Korean women who live under suppressed feelings of shame, anger and agony in an isolated state of desperation. China must be held accountable by allowing the UN High Commissioner for Refugees unimpeded access to North Koreans in China.

Provisions of the North Korean Human Rights Act calling for the admission of North Korean refugees into the United States have been ignored. As a result, the recent State Department report on implementation of the Act's refugee provisions was required to make the admission that not a single North Korean refugee has been admitted to the United States since the Act's passage. Special Envoy Lefkowitz has publicly voiced his determination to ensure the rapid admission of some refugees into the United States, but we need to ensure that the numbers of North Koreans admitted will be sufficient to provide real relief to North Korean refugees.

While I commend the tremendous work done in the TIP report and the progress made in working with NGO's and other governments on trafficking, in my view, the Report glosses over the very human aspect of internal trafficking in China. I want to encourage the State Department to focus more attention on the human rights violations inherent in internal trafficking in China.

While we can commend China for taking steps in the right direction, there are some real fundamental structural and policy issues within China that have to be resolved before we will see real progress in fighting trafficking.

We need to see much more progress from the Chinese Government in rescuing these victims and prosecuting those responsible. This means engaging China more forcefully on building a society based on the rule of law. We also need to engage China on the very human and social evils of the one-child policy and encourage them to end this policy now.

PREPARED STATEMENT OF HON. STEVEN J. LAW, DEPUTY SECRETARY, U.S. DEPARTMENT OF LABOR, MEMBER, CONGRESSIONAL-EXECUTIVE COMMISSION ON CHINA

MARCH 6, 2006

Chairman Hagel and Co-Chairman Leach, I thank you for holding this hearing that highlights one of today's worst human rights tragedies—the trafficking of humans for labor and sexual exploitation. I also want to recognize Ambassador John Miller and Mr. Roger Plant, both colleagues who I have been fortunate to work with in the global effort to fight human trafficking.

This Commission's legislative mandate is to monitor China's compliance with or violation of human rights, and I am particularly honored to serve as an executive branch commissioner on this topic. The abolition of human trafficking is an Administration priority that captured my professional and personal interest.

President Bush has called human trafficking a "modern form of slavery" and fighting to end this horrible practice remains an important goal of this Administration.

Three years ago, President Bush made a pledge before the United Nation's General Assembly to support organizations that are rescuing victims of trafficking around the world and are providing them hope for a better future.

In January of this year, President Bush again demonstrated his commitment to this issue, signing into law the Trafficking Victims Protection Reauthorization Act (TVPRA). This Act strengthens U.S. efforts to combat trafficking in persons in the United States and abroad, and it places renewed emphasis on the need to halt the trafficking of workers into various forms of labor exploitation. In signing this Act, the President also called upon other nations to take actions against trafficking within their own borders.

In my own Department, we are engaged both domestically and internationally in efforts to combat trafficking in persons. These efforts build upon the Department of Labor's long history of working to protect and assist vulnerable workers. Since 1995, the Department of Labor has provided over $164 million to fund projects that help to combat trafficking in persons for the purpose of labor and commercial sexual exploitation. In fiscal year 2005 alone, the Department of Labor provided $38.4 million to fund 13 projects in 18 countries.

As we begin this hearing, I would like to make an important distinction between human smuggling and human trafficking, as both are significant issues for China. The issue of human smuggling refers to the consensual endorsement of individuals to be transported to another country by circumventing immigration control. These individuals usually pay large sums of money to be illegally transported out of China. What distinguishes trafficking from smuggling is the presence of deception, force, or coercion designed to entrap a person in forced servitude and deny his or her fundamental right to freedom.

Across the world, the transnational phenomenon of human trafficking involves both trafficking for sex and labor exploitation, with a majority of trafficking cases involving some form of forced labor. Individuals are often forced to toil in brutal conditions in sweatshops and other hidden workplaces.

We recognize, however, that in many ways the problem of trafficking in China is unique. While sex and labor trafficking exist in China, factors such as cultural norms, demographic transitions, social policies, and economic conditions make individuals and communities in the country vulnerable to other forms of internal and cross-border trafficking.

For example, we have learned of documented instances of trafficking for forced marriage and illegal adoption in China. Women and girls in rural communities who choose to migrate to urban centers with hopes for better economic opportunities are sometimes tricked by job recruiters, and find themselves forced into marriage or into positions of involuntary servitude.

Moreover, China's one-child policy has allegedly contributed to the internal trafficking and/or abduction of male infants so that families without boys can raise them as their own to continue the family line. Baby girls are also reportedly a target for traffickers who see foreign adoption as a lucrative business.

Given the enormous size of China's population, at 1.3 billion people, there is an urgent need to uncover the scale and confront the problem of trafficking. As migration within and outside the country continues, the problem of human trafficking has the potential to escalate greatly. This is no time to downplay the problem.

As long as human trafficking persists in China, this Commission will remain steadfast in making this issue a focus of its agenda. While the Government of China has recognized human trafficking as a problem, much more remains to be done.

We need to call on the Government of China, neighboring countries, international agencies, and nongovernmental organizations to produce reliable research and data on the nature and magnitude of trafficking so that better policies and programs can be designed and implemented that respond to the country's trafficking problem.

As China positions itself as a dynamic player in the global economy and we continue to expand our trade relations with the country, we must call upon the Government of China to work diligently and earnestly to eliminate this modern-day form of slavery.

A little over a year ago, I had the opportunity to visit one of DOL-funded trafficking projects in India, and it was heartbreaking for me to see the conditions under which some children work and to hear the stories of victims of sex trafficking. At the same time, I was encouraged to witness first-hand the impact of successful programs to help trafficking victims and to see the hope restored in the eyes of children who had been trafficked.

With this, I look forward to hearing the first-hand experience of our distinguished panelists and to learning how their organizations address the indefensible institution of trafficking of women and children in China. Thank you.

○

CPSIA information can be obtained at www.ICGtesting.com
Printed in the USA
LVOW070252060712

288910LV00013BE/57/P